KAFFE FASSETT'S
Quilts en Provence

featuring Roberta Horton • Mary Mashuta • Liza Prior Lucy • Pauline Smith • Brandon Mably • Sally Davis • Ruth Eglinton • Judy Baldwin

A ROWAN PUBLICATION

The Taunton Press

The Taunton Press
Inspiration for hands-on living®

The Taunton Press, Inc., 63 South Main Street, PO Box 5506, Newtown, CT 06470-5506
email: tp@taunton.com

First published in Great Britain in 2010 by
Rowan Yarns
Green Lane Mill
Holmfirth
West Yorkshire
England
HD9 2DX

Art director:	Kaffe Fassett
Technical editors:	Ruth Eglinton and Pauline Smith
Co-ordinator:	Pauline Smith
Publishing consultant:	Susan Berry
Patchwork designs:	Kaffe Fassett, Roberta Horton, Mary Mashuta, Liza Prior Lucy, Pauline Smith, Brandon Mably, Judy Baldwin, Sally Davis, Ruth Eglinton
Quilters:	Judy Irish, Pauline Smith
Stitchers for Liza Prior Lucy quilts:	Judy Baldwin, Corienne Kramer
Photography:	Debbie Patterson
Flat shotphotography:	Dave Tolson @ Visage
Styling:	Kaffe Fassett
Design Layout:	Christine Wood - Gallery of Quilts/cover
	Simon Wagstaff - instructions & technical information
Illustrations:	Ruth Eglinton
Feature:	Philip Jacobs

Library of Congress Cataloging-in-Publication Data

Kaffe Fassett's quilts en Provence / featuring Roberta Horton ... [et al.].
    p. cm. -- (Patchwork and quilting book ; no. 12)
  ISBN 978-1-60085-324-1
 1. Patchwork--Patterns. 2. Quilting--Patterns. I. Fassett, Kaffe. II. Horton, Roberta. III. Title:
Quilts en Provence.
  TT835.K342 2010
  746.46--dc22

              2010010615

Colour reproduction by Chroma Graphics (Overseas) Pte. Ltd
Printed and bound in Singapore by KHL. Printing Co. Pte. Ltd

contents

introduction

Years ago when I first came to live in England, I was taken to the magical countryside of Provence, in France. My mind was so over-stimulated by the stone villages perched on hillsides with their cobbled streets and sumptuous lavender fields that I all but missed one of the real treasures of this area. I only glimpsed a row of houses as I rushed past Roussillon. That village is entirely red and ochre I was told and those words reverberated in my head over the years as I became more and more obsessed with colour in my work and searched locations to show it to best advantage.

You soon learn that highly coloured environments are thin on the ground, once you start looking. With those words, "red and ochre" in my head, I drove with my editor, Pauline Smith, photographer Debbie Patterson and assistant Brandon Mably more than 600 miles from London to see if possibly any of that colour still existed. Well, imagine my uncontained excitement as I spied the red buildings high on a hill across the Provençal landscape! As we wound our way up the hill past rich cliffs of blood red and gold ochre to find our gorgeous village

FAR LEFT: The golden ochre of this church has a soft depth of colour almost like old suede.

RIGHT: The street leading up the hill from our hotel in Roussillion. A typical combination of red, pink and ochre that this town is justly famous for.

BELOW: The sun rises on this Provençal hill-top town confident in its preservation.

BELOW RIGHT: This dramatic cliff of ochre rock dominates the view from the town centre, its rich colouring deepening in the evening and morning light.

even more richly coloured that I could have imagined. God bless the French for recognizing and preserving their heritage. We were so spoiled for choice in the one village we didn't need to go much further to do the entire book. Those reds went from softest shell pinks through to deep chestnut tone; the ochres ran from chamois leather shades of buff through to dark ambers, all set off by shutters of soft green, lavender and sky blue. I was so over the moon that even two rainy days didn't dampen my spirits. Colour so saturated and varied in an entire town, coupled with ancient buildings and winding streets on a hill, is a combo rare indeed.

I think you will agree that our quilts come to life in these elegant settings, making this one of our most memorable shoots. Our hotel and meals lived up to the occasion, too. As we sipped our rosé wine and toasted our day's shoot, thank goodness, I thought, that the words "that village is entirely red and ochre" stayed in my head, and how rewarding that the French have kept it that way.

ABOVE: What is it about painted surfaces and rambling vines that gives such pleasure.

BELOW LEFT: A corner of the ochre mine where so much of that raw pigment is obtained for paints.

BELOW: A lovely overgrown corner of Roussillon, with its beautiful pinky rust shutters and ancient grape vines.

THIS PAGE: Proof, if it were needed, how life enhancing colour is on these classic old French buildings: soft yet dancing with *joie de vivre*. How monochrome most towns are these days!

the fabrics

Mirage Stripe
by Kaffe Fassett (far left)

Caucasian Kelim carpets have always fascinated me with their dense repeating patterns. One of my favourite aspects of them is the way they weave interlocking contrast colours. The fabric printer did a splendid job of reproducing my fine points in this design. This stripe works a treat as a border and binding for quilts.

Embroidered Shawl
by Kaffe Fassett (left)

I've always loved the bold, up-scaled embroidered flowers on Chinese and Spanish shawls. I find the big, flat flowers really effective. It's fascinating how much each colourway changes in mood.

Sprays by Kaffe Fassett (right)

The world of oriental carpets is filled with handsome motifs that I've used in my needlepoint and knit designs. The stylized way they depict flowers is perfect for patchworkers as the flat, round shapes read very well when cut.

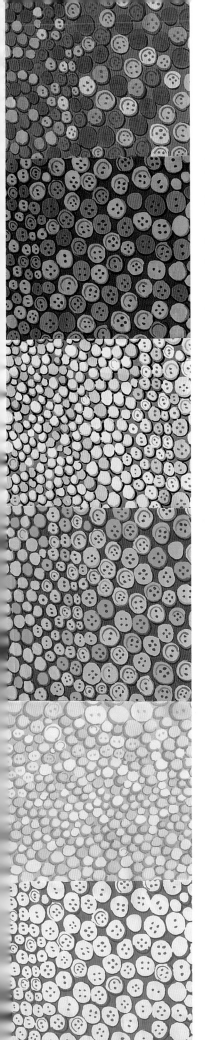

Buttons by Kaffe Fassett (left)

This is just a mad Polka dot that morphs into buttons. The design was inspired by the Pearly Kings and Queens of London, who spend years sewing pearl buttons onto black outfits. The dazzling costumes are worn in London parades. I make many embroideries and hats using buttons in homage to this historic idea, and love the look of a sheet of buttons in different scales.

Suzani by Kaffe Fassett (right)

The embroidered look of Suzani circles with all their variations are perfect for patchwork. I lined these circles up in a grid so you can cut very long rows of them as borders. Imagine using them as sashings in an all-over circular quilt.

Persian Vase
by Kaffe Fassett (far right)

Persian carpets often use rows of small flower forms to create an intense field of detail. I noticed they often start with a small decorative vase with a fountain of flower stems exploding out of it. With these bouquets of small blossoms you get an all-over composition of little circular forms that goes well with Buttons, Millefiore, Paperweight and Roman Glass. My *Persian Garden Quilt* uses all these fabrics with circular motifs to create a complex dottiness.

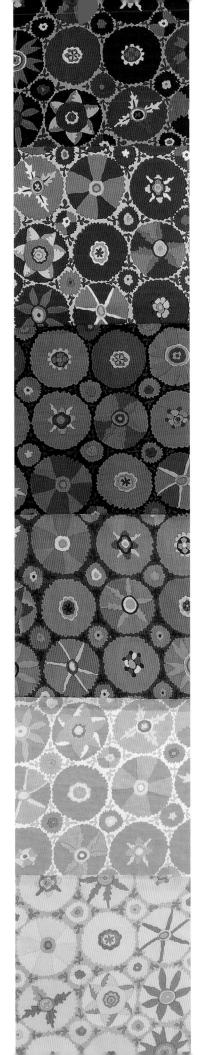

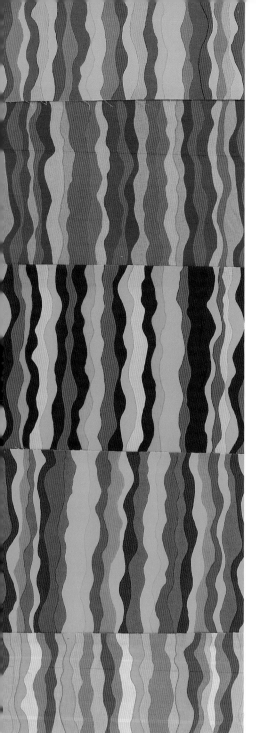

Fish Lips by Brandon Mably (below)

Brandon did a very loose decoration on a stoneware plate and the doughnut shapes suggested a fabric to him. He had a very successful shirt made of this print and really loves the way it adds such a free-form circle motif to the growing collection of circular elements in the Kaffe Collective.

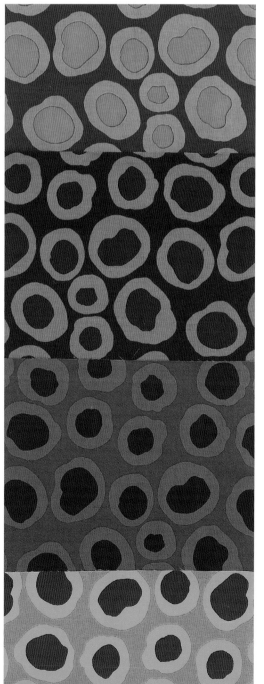

Waves by Brandon Mably (above)

In the quilter's vocabulary there always seem to be stripes of some sort, their lines contrasting with the roundness of flower forms. Because some quilters get quite rigid and nervous about matching up stripes precisely, Brandon thought he'd do a lovely organic stripe that enjoys not being precisely joined.

Straws by Brandon Mably (above)

Another very useful stripe, a little like shirt striping or jaunty ribbons. It is wonderful as sashing or any place where a soft striping is needed.

Scales by Brandon Mably (left)

Klimt, the great Austrian decorative painter, handed this idea to Brandon on a plate. It was the background for one of his portraits and cuts up a treat in patchwork arrangements. It makes gorgeous random borders and becomes quite leaf-like when paired with floral fabrics.

Tents by Brandon Mably (right)

This fine little geometric is seen in so many cultures from American Indian to ancient Egyptian. It has a bit of a tweedy texture when viewed from far off.

Garden Party by Philip Jacobs (left)
This is one of Philip Jacobs' most lush and celebratory of prints. The blossoms explode with joy, even the foliage seems to be doing a tipsy dance. I could just visualize a gorgeous summer party with lots of boozy punch making everyone happy and jigging about.

Waltzing Matilda by Philip Jacobs (right)
You might have noticed I love circular forms in quilts. This anemone with its big circular movement works so well when combined with more abstract circular prints. It has such movement I named it after the Australian song Waltzing Matilda since the flowers really dance to my eye.

Layered Leaves by Philip Jacobs (below)
When I was looking through Philip Jacobs' collection of possible patterns for this season I spotted this fresh leaf pattern and it reminded me pleasantly of old book covers or end papers. I felt it would be very useful for patchwork if it was coloured in a tonal fashion so you get a definite bias to each colourway. So it has proved. It is a good complement to the painterly lively florals in the collection.

Glory Rose by Philip Jacobs (above)
I chose this opulent full-blown rose print from the Philip Jacob's archive because I knew it would be so useful with its lush roses and verdant leaves. The all-over packed texture make it work so well for both traditional and more free-form quilters.

Summer Trees by Philip Jacobs (above)
We like to include some of the classic Arts and Crafts period fabrics in the Kaffe Collective and this fruit tree filled with birds is a rich addition to our palette. The yellow and pink colourways are particularly successful to me. It's a great honour to be able to apply my colour sense to these beautiful old prints.

philip jacobs: a passion for floral fabrics

I have always been a very visual person. I love looking at things: plant forms, trees looming out of the mist on a rainy day, the first snow of winter on a distant hill, the Milky Way stretching across the sky on a summer night, the first glimpse of the sea, blue and sparkling under the summer sun, the first berries and browning leaves in the hedgerows while the autumn sky turns a pale turquoise. When I visit anyone's house for the first time I always wander around looking at all their pictures and books, and any ornaments, then out into the garden to look at the plants. I just can't stop looking – it's something to do with the wonder of everything.

My early career

At school I didn't really know what was going on in the lessons half the time, but I loved painting. I would spend endless weekends when I was away at boarding school copying Japanese landscape prints by Hiroshige and Hokusai. Then, in the holidays, I would go up to the Victoria and Albert museum in London where I would examine the oriental collections and draw pictures of the Chinese porcelain and learn the Chinese and Japanese characters and date marks.

   Career-wise, I went through different phases when I thought I wanted to be a farmer, then a soldier, then an explorer, then an archaeologist and then an antique dealer before finally settling on being an artist. It was the thing I was best at and loved the most. When I went to art college I knew that I wanted to earn my living by painting but I wasn't sure how. But then one of my tutors, looking at my copies of Tibetan Thangka paintings, said, "I think we have a rare phenomenon here – a man who would be good at textiles". I gulped a bit as I had no interest at all in textiles, but I worked on a textile project and did well. After that, I did my degree in printed textiles, although I actually spent most of my time out in the country painting landscapes which I would then, on my return, print onto fabric using the silk screen process.

It wasn't until I left college that I really started designing fabrics in a big way, dividing my time between painting landscapes in the Isles of Scilly in the summer and working up fabric collections back in London through an agent for the US and UK dress and bed linen markets. I soon noticed that floral designs sold well so this became my speciality. As I painted different flowers, I found that I wanted to grow them as well, so this lead to an interest in gardening, which in turn fed back into my designs.

Burgeoning flowers

After a few years I turned my attention to the furnishing fabric market and worked freelance for many of the major UK furnishing houses including Sanderson, Liberty, G.P. & J. Baker, Warner, Osborne and Little, and Sekers among others. Eventually, in the late 1980s, I became design director of the old English fabric house: Ramm. Son & Crocker.

It was at the height of the fashion for English chintz, so as well as supplying our own outlets worldwide we also supplied most of the major US fabric houses such as Brunschwig & Fils, Lee Jofa, Rose Cummings, Baker furniture, Hinson and more. So great was the demand for our fabrics that I was often turning out two large furnishing designs a week and working way through the night just to keep up. But I was getting the reward of seeing the designs popping up in places as diverse as Hollywood movies or the decoration of the White House in the Clinton administration.

I've had always had a talent for finding old things: Japanese prints and oriental antiques in junk shops, dinosaur bones down by the sea, clay tobacco pipes along the Thames estuary. Now I turned my attention to building up a vast archive of antique textiles, wallpapers and botanical illustration from the 18th, 19th and 20th centuries, which in turn became a fantastic resource for my own designs. The particular period of textile and wallpaper design that interests me most is the second half of the 19th Century. It was the time of the Victorian plant hunters and they were bringing back new and exotic plants from distant lands.

These exotic blooms were soon reflected in the designs of the time. Up till about the 1840s floral design in textiles had been very stylized and largely influenced by the Indian "palampore" designs (hand-painted, mordant-dyed bedcovers) sent over by the East India Company, but from the mid-1840s there was an explosion of naturalistic floral design. The main exponents of this in England were the textile companies Thomas Clarkson and Stead McAlpin who were responsible for the traditional English floral chintz style. In France there were the companies Thierry-Mieg and Schwartz Huguenin, the latter employing the great designer Jean Ulric Tournier, who was noted for his sumptuous designs of dense bouquets and trails of beautifully painted plants.

It was this traditional floral style that most interested me, and that I developed in my work for Ramm's. Working from documentary textiles is also a fantastic way to hone one's technique. I feel that I'm continuing the great tradition of floral textiles that originated at that time. I was also developing my own more personal "transitional style". This involved the use of quite bold stylized flowers and leaves, particularly striped tulips, striped roses and picotee carnations along with banded poppies, edged anenomes, giant Japanese morning glories and exotic variegated leaves. It was a style I had previously used to good effect for Osborne & Little.

The Kaffe Fassett range

At different times throughout my career I've done collaborative work with Kaffe Fassett. We first met in 1973 and then in 1976 we worked together on a fabric collection for the Designers Guild. In 2004 we met up again seemingly by chance and Kaffe asked if I would be interested in designing for the patchwork quilt market. I took to it very rapidly. It was fantastic being able to use all the skill I had developed over the years designing furnishings, but in a new form. It feels very much as though I'm pouring the distilled essence of all that I've learned into these quilting collections for Westminster Fibers In my life the boundary between work and play has always been blurred, now it's just non-existent.

When I plan a collection of quilting fabric designs, I'm trying to achieve a balance of different scales and layouts, and a balance of traditional classic English florals and my own transitional style, usually comprising quite densely packed dramatic flowers and leaves. For inspiration I normally turn to my archive that is currently housed in an old stable at my home in Dorset. The walls are lined with stacks of old fabrics and boxes of ancient dusty wallpapers.

Sometimes I will select a document and redraw it virtually without any change, merely adapting it to fit the quilting fabric repeat sizes. At other times I will take the layout of one design and the flowers from another and create a new design. Sometimes I will blend

several different designs together. With each collection I'm trying to outdo myself: to take a previously successful layout but then to take it further: make it more sumptuous, more beautiful, more dramatic. That's the way designing develops – you have to work through and explore various different stages and styles. Then every design is a stage in a continuing process.

The more designs I produce the more the ideas seem to flow. It's always a great mystery where the ideas come from; I think there must be a great invisible ocean of inspiration somewhere and every so often a little bit of it becomes manifest. On some days the inspiration flows like a great torrent. Then I just jot the ideas down as a quick rough drawing and pin it to a board in my studio, where it awaits its turn to be painted up in full colour. Once I've painted up the design I look at it and think, "Gosh, where did that come from?" – it's as if I'm just a vehicle for its expression.

All the designs are painted by hand using water-colour paper, gouache paint, pencils, brushes and tracing paper. I don't use computers at all in the design process, though I do use a photocopier to help plan the layouts and to check the repeat once the design is complete. Once I feel I've produced enough designs that I'm pleased with I meet up with Kaffe, usually in London, to make the final selection (I call this "Kaffe's Christmas"). I paint the designs up in the main documentary or "natural" colour way, and Kaffe then works up a number of other colour ways to co-ordinate with his own collections.

Once the collection is complete and handed over I'm usually desperate to get on with the next group. Though I might also go off down to the beach to look for dinosaur relics or pursue another of my interests such as writing or antique hunting – activities which in a strange way refresh me for further designing. The key to being very happy in daily life, I feel, is to be passionate about lots of different things. Then life is a series of delights and you are always excited about waking up in the morning.

Several months after I've handed the collection over I get another treat: a big box arrives full of lengths of the newly printed designs (I should call this: "Philip's Christmas"!). It is just great unfolding length after length of freshly printed fabric. I also get further treats later on when I see pictures of the fantastic quilts and clothes that people have made using my designs.

The American mythologist Joseph Campbell who taught at Sarah Lawrence College in New York had a phrase that he used to tell his students – "follow your bliss". He explained how if you had the courage to do so, then you would find yourself on a track in life that had been there waiting for you all along. He said that you would then meet people who were in the field of your bliss and doors would open for you in place you didn't even know doors would be. That's been my experience exactly!

Aqua Panels by Kaffe Fassett

Imagine the thrill of stepping out onto our hotel terrace to be faced with this tapestry of lichen-covered tiles! The grey-green tones work so well with the *Aqua Panels Quilt.*

Persian Garden by Kaffe Fassett

The steps of this custard-toned building make a sunny backdrop for the high pastels in my *Persian Garden Quilt*.

Blush by Pauline Smith

The cool celadon shutters and apricot walls of Roussillon's central building bring out the best in Pauline's glowing quilt.

23

Enclosed Four Patch by
Roberta Horton

Roberta's strong quilt, full of
exuberance, certainly packs a
punch. This tiled entranceway
frames it perfectly.

Fruit Salad by Liza Prior Lucy

An old peeling wagon has just the right colours to
show off this confection of a quilt.

Game Board by Liza Prior Lucy

The powerful structure of Liza's contrasting quilt is complemented by the
theatrically painted door and carved stone.

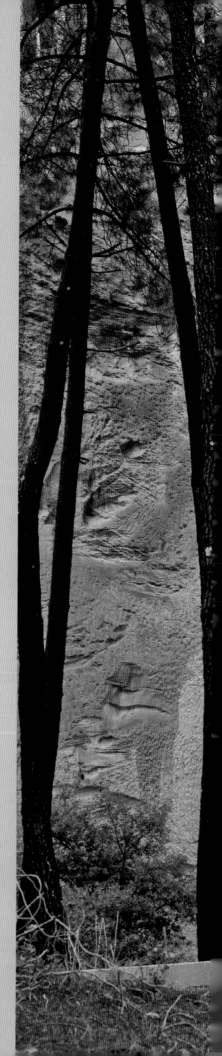

Lightning by Kaffe Fassett

The rich ochre cave entrance brings out the warmth in the marquetry-inspired patchwork of this quilt.

Mexican Party by Kaffe Fassett

The joyous pinks, oranges and yellows of this quilt dance
on the tangerine walls of this unique town.

Cheerful Party by
Mary Mashuta

What a celebration of
yellows in Mary's quilt
on the steps of this
church!

Sashed Boxes by Kaffe Fassett

This twist on Tumbling Boxes is usually done in hexagon shapes. The sashing makes it look as if the blocks are floating.

Secret Forest by
Pauline Smith

This joyous child's painting
of a quilt looks very much
at home on this bench in
front of a village house. The
sharp cobalt and magenta
shades are enhanced by the
Kelly green bench and *eau
de nil* shutters.

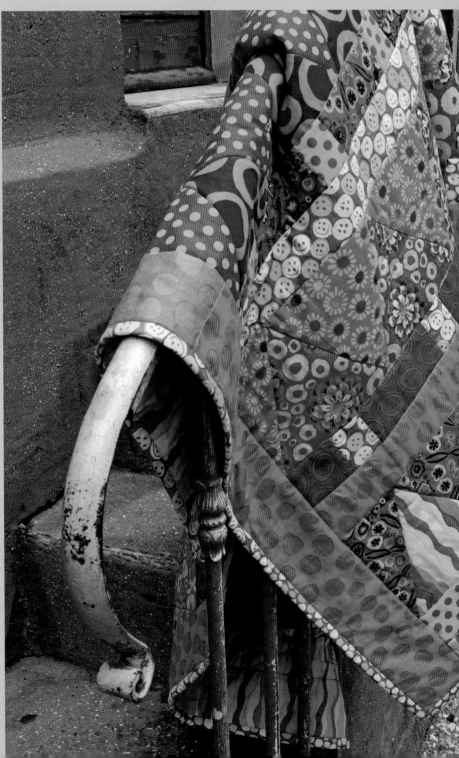

Sherbert by Ruth Eglinton

The candy coloured pastels of Ruth's charming quilt simply sparkle against the mustard wall (right) and also look just at home with the old lace and weathered shutters (left).

Snips and Snails by Sally Davis

The richly distressed texture of these walls echoes the complex, earthy palette of Sally's 16-patch quilt.

Sugar and Spice by Liza Prior Lucy

The cool palette and simple structure of this quilt is so at home against the bold stripes of the plaster on this building.

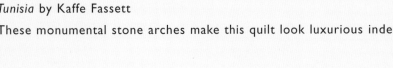

Tunisia by Kaffe Fassett
These monumental stone arches make this quilt look luxurious indeed.

X-Factor by Kaffe Fassett
The way simple diagonal striped blocks create such a complexity of shapes never ceases to astound me. The bold Picasso-like palette is so at home on these warm tones.

Beyond the Border by
Brandon Mably

Brandon's bold banner-like
quilt showcases his fabrics
excitingly. The southern
French light lends it a glow.

Fused Flowers on Target by Judy Baldwin

The unusual and interesting palette of Judy's quilt looks like it was made for this ochre wall – with the dramatic hill town of Gorde in the background.

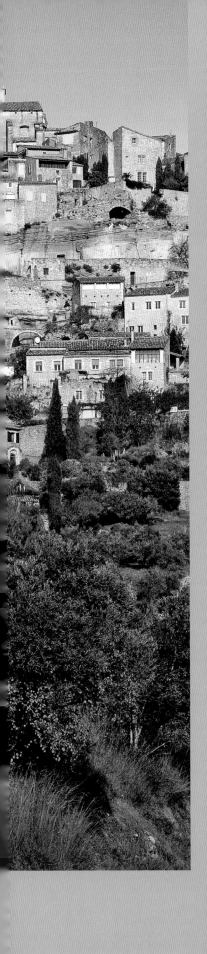

Porch Weave by Kaffe Fassett

The cool blues and magentas in this interesting, structured quilt responds really well to the ochre and terracotta of this old wall.

Yellow Panels by Kaffe Fassett

As fresh as spring daffodils this delicious yellow quilt, with its ribbon-like sashing, glows in the backlit village street.

Yellow Panels Quilt ★ ★

KAFFE FASSETT

The inspiration for this bright sunny quilt was a vintage quilt I kept coming across that used fussy cut flowers on white back grounds that had a very fresh look because of the space around each flower. I tried to create that effect by picking flowers on yellow grounds and extending those grounds with shot cotton borders. Brandon's Straws stripe fabric is like a fresh ribbon as a sashing.

SIZE OF QUILT
The finished quilt will measure approx.
92½in x 92½in (235cm x 235cm).

MATERIALS
Patchwork Fabrics:
Extra fabric has been allowed for fussy
cutting this quilt.
STRAWS
Pastel   BM08PT: 2¾yds (2.5m)
LAKE BLOSSOMS
Yellow   GP93YE: ¾yd (70cm)
RUSSIAN ROSE
Yellow   GP95YE: ¾yd (70cm)
GARDEN PARTY
Yellow   PJ20YE: ¾yd (70cm)
GLORY ROSE
Magenta   PJ21MG: ¾yd (70cm)
DELPHINIUM
Yellow   PJ25YE: ⅝yd (60cm)
SUMMER TREE
Yellow   PJ27YE: ¾yd (70cm)

FLORAL BURST
Yellow   PJ29YE: ¾yd (70cm)
DAFFODILS AND DOGWOOD
Yellow   PJ31YE: ⅝yd (60cm)
SHOT COTTON
Lemon   SC34: 3¼yds (3m)

Backing Fabric: 7¾yds (7.1m)
We suggest these fabrics for backing:
SUMMER TREE Yellow, PJ27YE
FLORAL BURST Yellow, PJ29YE

Binding:
GLORY ROSE
Magenta PJ21MG: ⅞yd (80cm)

Batting:
100in x 100in (254cm x 254cm).

Quilting Thread:
Toning machine quilting thread.

Templates:

W   X   V

PATCH SHAPES
The floral squares in this quilt (Template W)
are carefully fussy cut to centre on the
blooms in the fabric designs. Each square is
then surrounded, 'courthouse steps' style with
framing strips (cut to size). The framed blocks
are then set 'on point' interspaced with
sashing strips (cut to size) and corner posts
(fussy cut to size). The ends of the rows and
the corners of the quilt centre are completed
with 2 triangle patch shapes (Templates X
and V), which again have framing strips. The
completed quilt centre is then surrounded by
a simple border. We recommend using

Block Assembly Diagrams

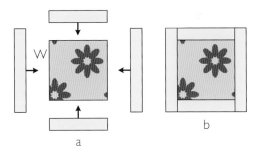

a   b

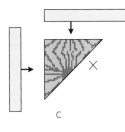   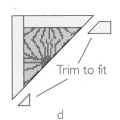   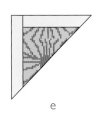

c   d   e

f   g   h

Quilt Assembly Diagram

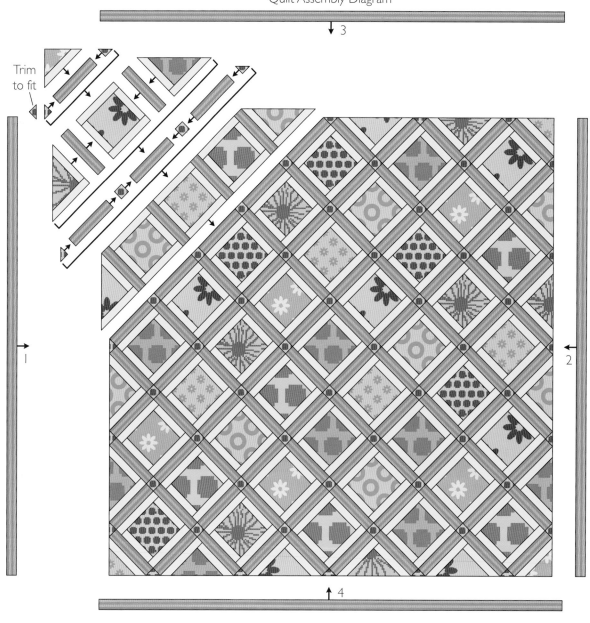

Trim to fit

3

1

2

4

= BM08PT	= PJ21MG	= PJ31YE	
= GP93YE	= PJ25YE	= SC34	
= GP95YE	= PJ27YE		
= PJ20YE	= PJ29YE		

transparent plastic for template W to make fussy cutting the blooms easier.

CUTTING OUT

Our usual 'strip cutting' method is not suitable for cutting the template W squares and template X and V triangles in the large floral fabrics. We recommend drawing out the shapes onto the fabric before cutting to prevent waste.

Template X: Cut 11⅞in (30.25cm) squares (not fussy cut), cut each square twice diagonally to make 4 triangles using the template as a guide, this will ensure that the long side of the triangles will not have a bias edge. Note: Do not move the patches until both diagonals have been cut. Cut 4 triangles in GP93YE, PJ20YE, PJ27YE and PJ29YE.
Template W: Cut 8in (20.25cm) squares centred on the large blooms in the fabric designs (see the photograph for details). Cut 6 in GP95YE, PJ29YE, 5 in PJ20YE, PJ21MG, PJ25YE, PJ27YE, PJ31YE and 4 in GP93YE.
Template V: Cut 6¼in (16cm) squares (not fussy cut), cut each square diagonally once to make 2 triangles. Cut 2 triangles in PJ25YE and PJ31YE.
Sashing Posts: Cut 2½in (6.5cm) squares centred on the blooms in the fabric design. Cut 60 in PJ21MG. Choose the best 40 squares for the centre of the quilt and use the remaining 20 around the edges where they will be trimmed to triangles after the rows are pieced.
Short Framing Strips: Cut 8in (20.25cm) strips across the width of the fabric. Each strip will give you 20 patches per full width. Cut 82 strips 2in x 8in (5cm x 20.25cm) in SC34.
Long Framing Strips: Cut 11in (28cm) strips across the width of the fabric. Each strip will give you 20 patches per full width. Cut 118 strips 2in x 11in (5cm x 28cm) in SC34. 82 strips are used for framing the template W squares and the remaining 36 are used with the template X and V triangles.
Borders: Open out and cut this fabric very carefully down the length keeping the stripes straight. Cut 2 strips 2½in x 94in (6.5cm x 238.75cm) for the quilt top and bottom and 2 strips 2½in x 90in (6.5cm x 228.5cm) for the quilt sides in BM08PT. These are a little oversized and will be trimmed to fit exactly later.
Sashing: From the remaining BM08PT fabric cut very carefully down the length keeping the stripes straight. Cut100 strips 2½in x 11in (6.5cm x 28cm).

Binding: Cut 10 strips 2½in (6.5cm) wide across the width of the fabric in PJ21MG.

Backing: Cut 2 pieces 40in x 100in (101.5cm x 254cm) 2 pieces 40in x 21in (101.5cm x 53.25cm) and 1 piece 21in x 21in (53.25cm x 53.25cm) in backing fabric.

MAKING THE BLOCKS

Use a ¼in (6mm) seam allowance throughout. Take the fussy cut template W squares and add framing strips as shown in block assembly diagram a, the framed block can be seen in diagram b, make 41. Take the template X triangles and add framing strips to the 2 short sides as shown in diagram c. Trim the strips to fit as shown in diagram d, the finished block can been seen in diagram e, make 16. Take the template V triangles and a framing strip to the long side as shown in diagram f. Trim the strip to fit as shown in diagram g, the finished block can been seen in diagram h, make 4.

MAKING THE QUILT

Refer to the quilt assembly diagram for fabric placement. Lay out the framed blocks interspaced with the sashing strips and sashing posts, fill in the edges and corners of the quilt with the triangular blocks and separate into diagonal rows as shown in the quilt assembly diagram. Piece the rows and then join them to form the quilt centre. Trim the sashing posts to fit the quilt edge ensuring you leave a ¼in (6mm) seam allowance. Add the side borders and trim to fit exactly, finally add the top and bottom borders and trim to fit exactly to complete the quilt.

FINISHING THE QUILT

Press the quilt top. Seam the backing pieces using a ¼in (6mm) seam allowance to form a piece approx. 100in x 100in (254cm x 254cm). Layer the quilt top, batting and backing and baste together (see page 139). Using toning machine quilting thread quilt all the framing and sashing seams in the ditch. Free motion meander quilt following the fabric designs in the template W squares. Trim the quilt edges and attach the binding (see page 140).

Aqua Panels Quilt ★★

KAFFE FASSETT

Aqua Panels shares the same layout as Yellow Panels. In this cool aqua version I've placed the blocks in diagonal rows of the same fabric for a very different look. This idea would work in many different colourings.

SIZE OF QUILT
The finished quilt will measure approx.
92½in x 92½in (235cm x 235cm).

MATERIALS
Patchwork Fabrics:
Extra fabric has been allowed for fussy cutting the PJ20JA, PJ23CD and GP59GN fabrics.
STRAWS
Rust   BM08RU: 2¾yds (2.5m)
GUINEA FLOWER
Green   GP59GN: ¾yd (70cm)
GARDEN PARTY
Jade   PJ20JA: 1yd (90cm)
GLORY ROSE
Blue   PJ21BL: ⅞yd (80cm)

WALTZING MATILDA
Emerald   PJ22ED: 1⅛yds (1m)
TROPICAL
Celadon   PJ23CD: 1yd (90cm)
SHOT COTTON
Aqua   SC77: 3¼yds (3m)

Backing Fabric: 7¾yds (7.1m)
We suggest these fabrics for backing:
GARDEN PARTY Jade, PJ20JA
GLORY ROSE Blue, PJ21BL
TROPICAL Celadon, PJ23CD

Binding:
GUINEA FLOWER
Green   GP59GN: ⅞yd (80cm)

Batting:
100in x 100in (254cm x 254cm).

Quilting Thread:
Toning machine quilting thread.

Templates:
See Yellow Panels Quilt.

PATCH SHAPES
See Yellow Panels Quilt instructions. Note: In this version of the quilt only the PJ20JA fabric and PJ23CD for template W and the GP59GN fabric for the sashing posts are fussy cut.

CUTTING OUT
Our usual 'strip cutting' method is not

suitable for cutting the template W squares and template X and V triangles in the large floral fabrics. We recommend drawing out the shapes onto the fabric before cutting to prevent waste.

Template X: Cut 11⅞in (30.25cm) squares, cut each square twice diagonally to make 4 triangles using the template as a guide, this will ensure that the long side of the triangles will not have a bias edge. Note: Do not move the patches until both diagonals have been cut. Cut 4 triangles in PJ20JA, PJ21BL, PJ22ED and PJ23CD.

Template W: Cut 8in (20.25cm) squares, Note only the PJ20JA and PJ23CD fabrics are fussy cut. Cut 11 in PJ22ED, 10 in PJ20JA, PJ21BL and PJ23CD.

Template V: Cut 6¼in (16cm) squares, cut each square diagonally once to make 2 triangles. Cut 2 triangles in PJ22ED, 1 in PJ20JA and PJ21BL.

Sashing Posts: Cut 2½in (6.5cm) squares centred on the blooms in the fabric design. Cut 60 in GP59GN. Choose the best 40

squares for the centre of the quilt and use the remaining 20 around the edges where they will be trimmed to triangles after the rows are pieced.

Short Framing Strips: Cut 8in (20.25cm) strips across the width of the fabric. Each strip will give you 20 patches per full width. Cut 82 strips 2in × 8in (5cm × 20.25cm) in SC77.

Long Framing Strips: Cut 11in (28cm) strips across the width of the fabric. Each strip will give you 20 patches per full width. Cut 118 strips 2in × 11in (5cm × 28cm) in SC77. 82 strips are used for framing the template W squares and the remaining 36 are used with the template X and V triangles.

Borders: Open out and cut this fabric very carefully down the length keeping the stripes straight. Cut 2 strips 2½in × 94in (6.5cm × 238.75cm) for the quilt top and bottom and 2 strips 2½in × 90in (6.5cm × 228.5cm) for the quilt sides in BM08RU. These are a little oversized and will be trimmed to fit exactly later.

Sashing: From the remaining BM08RU fabric cut very carefully down the length keeping

the stripes straight. Cut 100 strips 2½in × 11in (6.5cm × 28cm).

Binding: Cut 10 strips 2½in (6.5cm) wide across the width of the fabric in GP59GN.

Backing: Cut 2 pieces 40in × 100in (101.5cm × 254cm) 2 pieces 40in × 21in (101.5cm × 53.25cm) and 1 piece 21in × 21in (53.25cm × 53.25cm) in backing fabric.

MAKING THE BLOCKS
See Yellow Panels Quilt instructions.

MAKING THE QUILT
See Yellow Panels Quilt instructions.

FINISHING THE QUILT
See Yellow Panels Quilt instructions.
Note: Using toning machine quilting thread quilt all the framing and sashing seams in the ditch. Free motion meander quilt following the fabric designs or hand quilt a 3½in (9cm) square in the centre of the framed squares.

Quilt Assembly Diagram

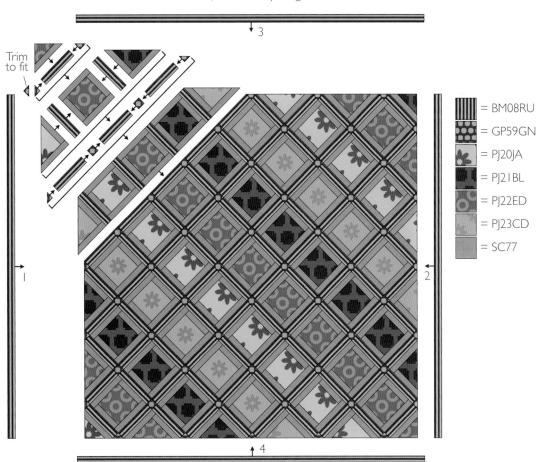

= BM08RU
= GP59GN
= PJ20JA
= PJ21BL
= PJ22ED
= PJ23CD
= SC77

Sherbet Quilt ★★★
RUTH EGLINTON

Hexagon quilts are fascinating and the idea of machine piecing one prompted Ruth to design this pretty quilt using Kaffe and Philip's brighter pastel fabrics. The Shot Cottons blend so well with the prints and by choosing colour elements that occur in several of the prints it ties the whole palette together. This would be an easy quilt to re-colour, perhaps in rich reds or autumn colours. Ruth used the foundation method as the bias edges of the triangles and hexagons make piecing tricky!

SIZE OF QUILT
The finished quilt will measure approx. 36in x 48½in (91.5cm x 123cm).

MATERIALS
Patchwork and Border Fabrics:
ASIAN CIRCLES
Green   GP89GN: ⅜yd (35cm)
Pink   GP89PK: ⅜yd (35cm)
MILLEFIORE
Pastel   GP92PT: ⅜yd (35cm)
LAKE BLOSSOMS
Green   GP93GN: ⅜yd (35cm)
PERSIAN VASE
Duck Egg   GP100DE: ⅜yd (35cm)
SPRAYS
Taupe   GP107TA: ⅜yd (35cm)
WALTZING MATILDA
Pastel   PJ22PT: ⅜yd (35cm)
LAYERED LEAVES
Celadon   PJ26CD: ⅜yd (35cm)
SHOT COTTON
Lavender   SC14: ¼yd (25cm)
Watermelon   SC33: ¼yd (25cm)
Lilac   SC36: ¼yd (25cm)
Apple   SC39: ¼yd (25cm)
Jade   SC41: ¼yd (25cm)
Pudding   SC68: ¼yd (25cm)
Pink   SC83: ¼yd (25cm)

Backing Fabric: 2yds (1.8m)
We suggest these fabrics for backing:
SPOT Lavender, GP70LV
ASIAN CIRCLES Pink, GP89PK
LAKE BLOSSOMS Green, GP93GN

Binding:
SPOT
Lavender   GP70LV: ½yd (45cm)

Batting:
44in x 56in (112cm x 142.5cm).

Quilting Thread:
Toning hand quilting thread.

Templates:

This quilt also uses the Foundation Patterns printed on page 126

PATCH SHAPES
This hexagon quilt is foundation pieced. The fabrics are pre-cut into 1 rectangle shape (cut to size) and 1 triangle shape for which we have provided a cutting template (Template A), this is oversized to allow for easy foundation piecing. The main blocks (Foundation Pattern B) are pieced into vertical rows. The row ends are completed with 2 further blocks (Foundation Patterns C and D).

CUTTING OUT
Template A: Cut 3½in (9cm) strips across the width of the fabric. Each strip will give you 18 patches per full width. Cut 32 in SC33, 31 in SC41, 28 in SC36, 26 in SC14, SC39, 25 in SC68 and 22 in SC83, these triangles are oversized to allow for easy foundation piecing.

Rectangles for Foundation Pattern B: Cut 4½in (11.5cm) strips across the width of the fabric. Each strip will give you 7 patches per full width. Cut 4½in x 5½in (11.5cm x 14cm) rectangles. Cut 12 in GP89GN, GP89PK, GP100DE, GP107TA, PJ22PT, 10 in GP92PT, 9 in GP93GN and 7 in PJ26CD. Reserve leftover fabric strips for Foundation Patterns C and D.

Binding: Cut 5 strips 2½in (6.5cm) wide across the width of the fabric in GP70LV.

Backing: Cut 1 piece 40in x 56in (101.5cm x 142.5cm), 1 piece 40in x 5in (101.5cm x 12.75cm) and 1 piece 17in x 5in (43.25cm x 12.75cm) in backing fabric.

MAKING THE BLOCKS

Foundation Piecing:
For the foundation piecing diagrams RS = right side, WS = wrong side. The foundation papers are divided into numbered sections, this is the order in which fabric pieces are added. Trace or photocopy then cut out 86 copies of Foundation Pattern B, 8 copies of Foundation Pattern C and 10 copies of Foundation Pattern D (you may wish to make extra copies for practice). The thinnest 'bank' paper or low quality photocopy paper works well.

Stage 1: Using the quilt assembly diagram as a guide for fabric placement, select a 4½in x 5½in (11.5cm x 14cm) rectangle and line it up with the wrong side of the fabric against the back of a foundation pattern B as shown in the stage 1 diagram. Pin the fabric to the paper placing the pins in the positions shown, away from the dotted stitching lines.

Stage 2: Turn the foundation paper face down. Select 2 shot cotton triangles and line them up, right sides together, with the edges of the rectangle as shown. Pin each triangle in place.

Stage 3: Turn the foundation paper face up again and stitch the 2 sewing lines, extending the lines to the edges of the triangles as shown.

Stage 4: Remove all the pins and open out the 2 triangles, press without using steam as it can wrinkle the paper. Place the block fabric side down and carefully trim to the solid outer line.

Stage 5: Flip the block over to see the completed block. Don't remove the papers yet.

Use the same method to piece the foundation pattern C and D blocks, using the leftover strips of print fabrics and 1 shot cotton triangle for each.

MAKING THE QUILT
Arrange the B blocks into 9 vertical rows, using the C and D blocks to complete the row ends as shown in the quilt assembly diagram. Join the blocks into rows, you will need to offset the blocks so that the seams intersect at the correct position as shown in the stage 6 diagram. Join the rows, offsetting the rows in the same way to complete the quilt. Finally, you can remove the papers!

FINISHING THE QUILT
Press the quilt top. Seam the backing pieces using a ¼in (6mm) seam allowance to form a piece approx. 44in x 56in (112cm x 142.5cm). Layer the quilt top, batting and backing and baste together (see page 139). Using toning hand quilting thread, quilt ⅜in (1cm) inside the seam in each hexagon shape. Trim the quilt edges and attach the binding (see page 140).

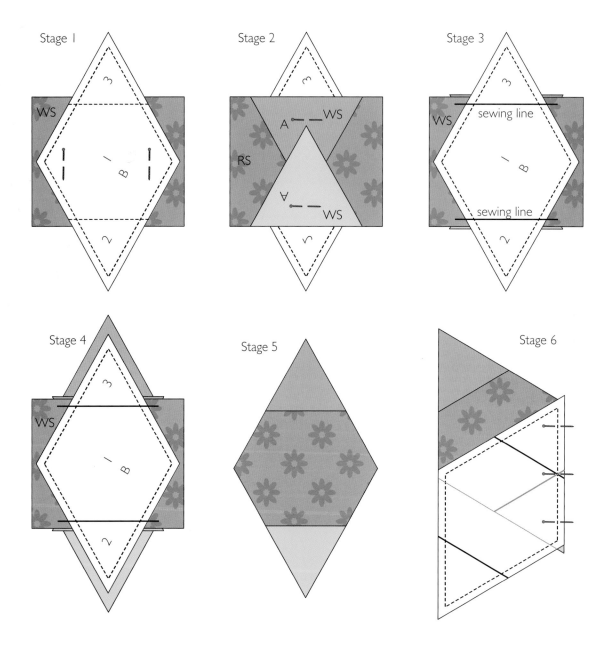

Stage 1

Stage 2

Stage 3

Stage 4

Stage 5

Stage 6

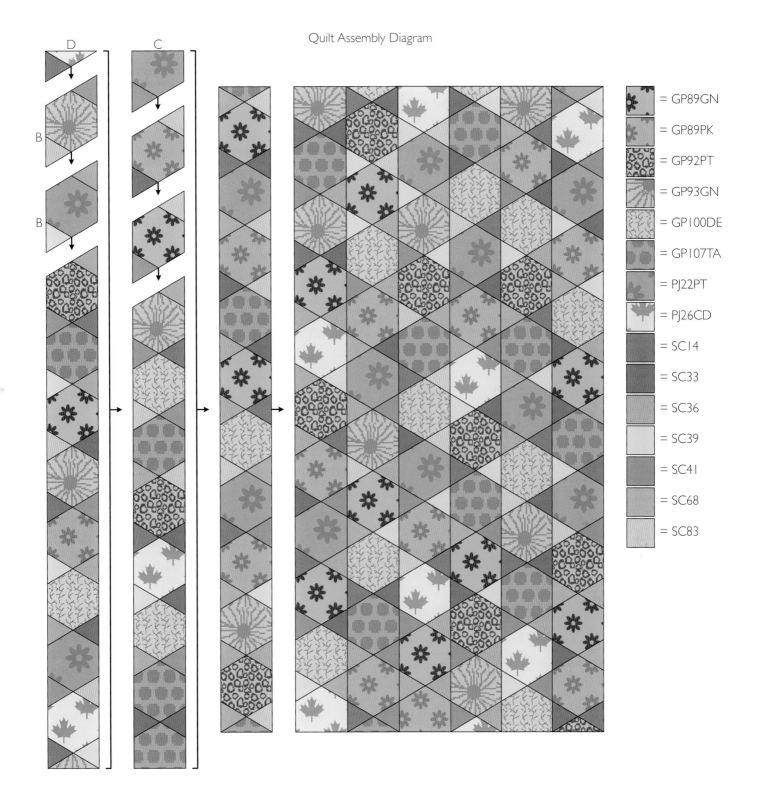

= GP89GN

= GP89PK

= GP92PT

= GP93GN

= GP100DE

= GP107TA

= PJ22PT

= PJ26CD

= SC14

= SC33

= SC36

= SC39

= SC41

= SC68

= SC83

Sugar and Spice Quilt ★

LIZA PRIOR LUCY

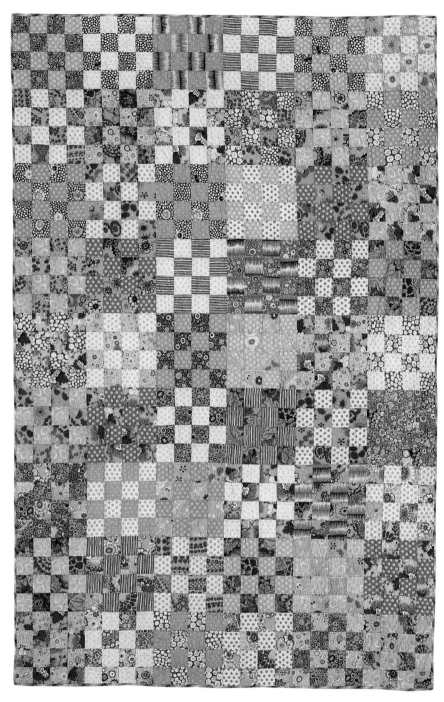

In 1993 Liza bought a painting. The entire Rowan Patchwork and Quilting Company came about because of that painting. It is a still life that Kaffe painted in the late 1970s of a pastel quilt and antique containers. He sold it to an American woman living in London. She eventually moved back to America and wanted to sell the painting by Kaffe. Through the grapevine she heard that Liza might want to purchase a painting by Kaffe. Indeed, Liza did want it. Only a few months earlier Liza had tried to convince Kaffe to do a patchwork book together and he wasn't too keen on the idea. When he learned that Liza had possession of his painting, he thought it was an omen that they should do the quilt book that she had proposed. Here is Liza's interpretation of the quilt in the painting she bought, 15 years later.

SIZE OF QUILT
The finished quilt will measure approx.
60in × 90in (152.5cm × 228.5cm).

MATERIALS
We have drawn the quilt showing the exact placement Liza used, however this is meant to be a 'scrappy style' quilt and exact placement of fabrics are not important.

Patchwork Fabrics:

STRAWS
Pastel   BM08PT: ⅜yd (35cm)
ROMAN GLASS
Blue/White   GP01BW: ⅛yd (15cm)
Pink   GP01PK: ¼yd (25cm)
Pastel   GP01PT: ⅜yd (35cm)
PAPERWEIGHT
Sludge   GP20SL: ⅜yd (35cm)
CLOISONNE
Aqua   GP46AQ: ⅜yd (35cm)
GUINEA FLOWER
Blue   GP59BL: ⅜yd (35cm)
SPOT
Duck Egg   GP70DE: ⅜yd (35cm)
Hydrangea   GP70HY: ⅜yd (35cm)
Lavender   GP70LV: ⅜yd (35cm)
Magnolia   GP70MN: ¼yd (25cm)
Mint   GO70MT: ⅜yd (35cm)
Sky   GP70SK: ⅜yd (35cm)
Sprout   GP70SR: ⅜yd (35cm)
Taffy   GP70TF: ⅜yd (35cm)
Water   GP70WT: ⅜yd (35cm)
ABORIGINAL DOTS
Cream   GP71CM: ¼yd (25cm)
Sweet Pea   GP71SW: ⅜yd (35cm)
ASIAN CIRCLES
Green   GP89GN: ⅜yd (35cm)
Pink   GP89PK: ⅜yd (35cm)
MILLEFIORE
Pastel   GP92PT: ¼yd (25cm)
PERSIAN VASE
Duck Egg   GP100DE: ⅜yd (35cm)

BUTTONS
Blue   GP101BL: ⅜yd (35cm)
MIRAGE STRIPE
Blue   GP104BL: ¼yd (25cm)
SPRAYS
Lime   GP107LM: ⅜yd (35cm)
Turquoise   GP107TQ: ⅜yd (35cm)
LAYERED LEAVES
Celadon   PJ26CD: ⅜yd (35cm)
Blue   PJ26BL: ⅜yd (35cm)

Backing Fabric: 5¼yds (4.8m)
Any of the SPOT fabrics used in the quilt would be suitable for backing.

Binding:
MIRAGE STRIPE
Blue   GP104BL: ¾yd (70cm)

Batting:
68in × 98in (172.5cm × 249cm).

Quilting Thread:
Light pink machine quilting thread.

Templates:

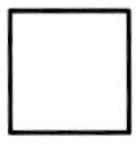

J

PATCH SHAPES
This quilt is pieced using a single square patch shape (Template J), the squares are pieced into simple blocks which are then set in simple rows, ideal for a beginner.

CUTTING OUT
Template J: Cut 3in (7.5cm) strips across the width of the fabric. Each strip will give you 13 patches per full width. Cut 40 in GP01PT, GP20SL, GP46AQ, GP70DE, GP70HY,

GP101BL, 32 in BM08PT, GP59BL, GP70LV, GP70MT, GP70SK, GP70SR, GP70TF, GP70WT, GP71SW, GP89GN, GP89PK, GP100DE, GP107LM, GP107TQ, PJ26CD, PJ26BL, 24 in GP70MN, GP71CM, GP104BL, 16 in GP01PK, GP92PT and 8 in GP01BW.

Binding: Cut 8⅝yds (7.9m) of 2½in (6.5cm) wide bias binding in GP104BL.

Backing: Cut 2 pieces 40in × 68in (101.5cm × 172.5cm), 1 piece 40in × 19in (101.5cm × 48cm) and 1 piece 29in × 19in (73.5cm × 48cm) in backing fabric.

MAKING THE QUILT
Use a ¼in (6mm) seam allowance throughout. This is a scrappy style quilt, it isn't necessary to place each fabric as in the original to achieve the same effect. Just choose two fabrics, one slightly lighter than the other for each block. Take 8 squares of each colour to make each block following block assembly diagram a. The finished block can be seen in diagram b. Make a total of 54 blocks. Arrange the blocks, each with the darker fabric in the top left corner, so that the checkerboard effect is consistent throughout the quilt, also arrange them so that the colours are well spread. Join the blocks into 9 rows of 6 blocks and then join the rows to complete the quilt.

FINISHING THE QUILT
Press the quilt top. Seam the backing pieces using a ¼in (6mm) seam allowance to form a piece approx. 68in × 98in (172.5cm × 249cm). Layer the quilt top, batting and backing and baste together (see page 139). Using light pink thread quilt free form flower and leaf shapes throughout. Trim the quilt edges and attach the binding (see page 140).

Block Assembly Diagrams

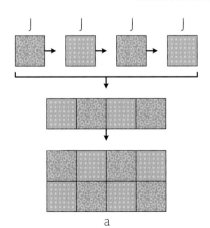

a

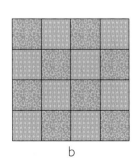

b

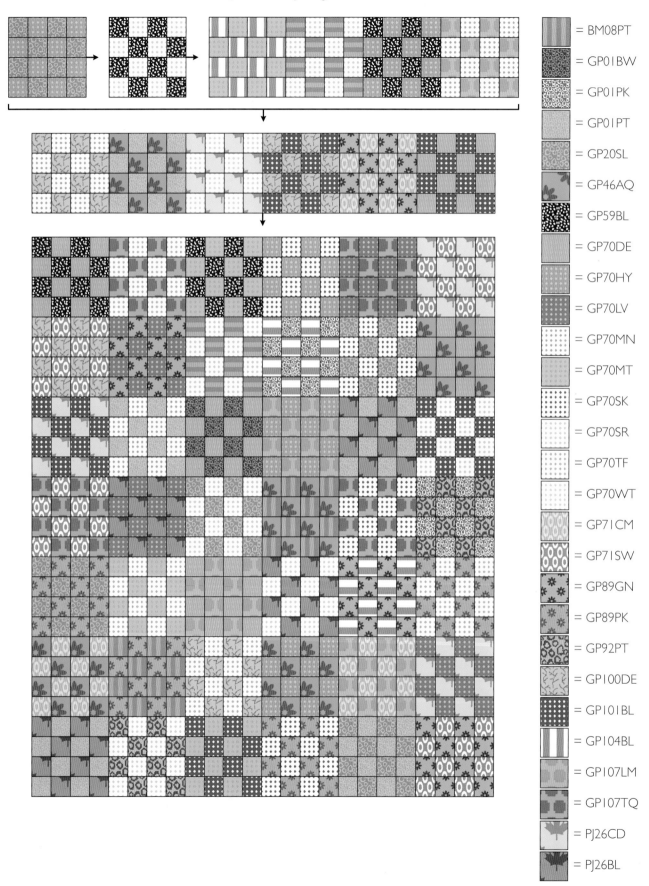

= BM08PT
= GP01BW
= GP01PK
= GP01PT
= GP20SL
= GP46AQ
= GP59BL
= GP70DE
= GP70HY
= GP70LV
= GP70MN
= GP70MT
= GP70SK
= GP70SR
= GP70TF
= GP70WT
= GP71CM
= GP71SW
= GP89GN
= GP89PK
= GP92PT
= GP100DE
= GP101BL
= GP104BL
= GP107LM
= GP107TQ
= PJ26CD
= PJ26BL

Snips and Snails Quilt ★

SALLY DAVIS

Liza thought it would be a great idea for Sally to take the same simple 16 patch layout as her pastel Sugar and Spice Quilt but give it a totally different palette. Sally selected rich earthy shades for her sumptuous quilt.

SIZE OF QUILT
The finished quilt will measure approx. 60in x 90in (152.5cm x 228.5cm).

MATERIALS
We have drawn the quilt showing the exact placement Sally used, however this is meant to be a 'scrappy style' quilt and exact placement of fabrics are not important.

Patchwork Fabrics:

STRAWS
Lime	BM08LM:	¼yd (25cm)
Rust	BM08RU:	¼yd (25cm)

ROMAN GLASS
Byzantine	GP01BY:	¼yd (25cm)
Gold	GP01GD:	¼yd (25cm)
Leafy	GP01LF:	¼yd (25cm)

PAPERWEIGHT
Pumpkin	GP20PN:	⅛yd (15cm)

GUINEA FLOWER
Yellow	GP59YE:	¼yd (25cm)

PAISLEY JUNGLE
Moss	GP60MS:	¼yd (25cm)
Purple	GP60PU:	¼yd (25cm)
Rust	GP60RU:	⅛yd (15cm)
Tangerine	GP60TN:	½yd (45cm)

TARGETS
Brown	GP67BR:	¼yd (25cm)

SPOT
Burgundy	GP70BG:	¼yd (25cm)
Red	GP70RD:	⅛yd (15cm)

ABORIGINAL DOTS
Chocolate	GP71CL:	¼yd (25cm)
Forest	GP71FO:	⅛yd (15cm)
Gold	GP71GD:	¼yd (25cm)
Leaf	GP71LF:	¼yd (25cm)
Ochre	GP71OC:	⅛yd (15cm)
Ocean	GP71ON:	⅜yd (35cm)
Orange	GP71OR:	¼yd (25cm)
Red	GP71RD:	⅜yd (35cm)

CHEVRON STRIPE
Ochre	GP90OC:	⅜yd (35cm)

MILLEFIORE
Brown	GP92BR:	¼yd (25cm)

PERSIAN VASE
Brown	GP100BR:	⅜yd (35cm)

BUTTONS
Brown	GP101BR:	⅜yd (35cm)

MIRAGE STRIPE
Brown	GP104BR:	½yd (45cm)

SUZANI
Black	GP105BK:	¼yd (25cm)

BEGONIA LEAVES
Cobalt	PJ18CB:	¼yd (25cm)

WALTZING MATILDA
Dark	PJ22DK:	¼yd (25cm)
Moss	PJ22MS:	¼yd (25cm)

TROPICAL
Emerald	PJ23ED:	¼yd (25cm)

TULIP MANIA
Blue	PJ24BL:	¼yd (25cm)
Green	PJ24GN:	⅜yd (35cm)

LAYERED LEAVES
Red	PJ26RD:	¼yd (25cm)

Backing Fabric: 5¼yds (4.8m)
We suggest these fabrics for backing:
LOTUS LEAF Green, GP29GN
Or any of the prints in the quilt.

Binding:
MIRAGE STRIPE
Brown	GP104BR:	¾yd (70cm)

Batting:
68in x 98in (172.5cm x 249cm).

Quilting Thread:
Toning machine quilting thread.

Templates:
See Sugar and Spice Quilt instructions.

PATCH SHAPES
See Sugar and Spice Quilt instructions.

CUTTING OUT
Template J: Cut 3in (7.5cm) strips across the width of the fabric. Each strip will give you 13 patches per full width. Cut 64 in GP104BR, 56 in GP60TN, 40 in GP101BR, 32 in GP71ON, GP71RD, GP90OC, GP100BR, PJ24GN, 24 in BM08LM, BM08RU, GP01BY, GP01GD, GP01LF, GP59YE, GP60MS, GP67BR, GP71GD, GP71LF, GP71OR, GP92BR, GP105BK, PJ18CB, PJ22DK, PJ22MS, PJ23ED, PJ24BL, PJ26RD, 16 in GP60PU, GP70BG, GP71CL, 8 in GP20PN, GP60RU, GP70RD, GP71FO and GP71OC.

Binding: Cut 8⅝yds (7.9m) of 2½in (6.5cm) wide bias binding in GP104BR.

Backing: Cut 2 pieces 40in x 68in (101.5cm x 172.5cm), 1 piece 40in x 19in (101.5cm x 48cm) and 1 piece 29in x 19in (73.5cm x 48cm) in backing fabric.

MAKING THE QUILT
See Sugar and Spice Quilt instructions.

FINISHING THE QUILT
Press the quilt top. Seam the backing pieces using a ¼in (6mm) seam allowance to form a piece approx. 68in x 98in (172.5cm x 249cm). Layer the quilt top, batting and backing and baste together (see page 139). Using toning thread quilt free form flower and leaf shapes throughout. Trim the quilt edges and attach the binding (see page 140).

Quilt Assembly Diagram

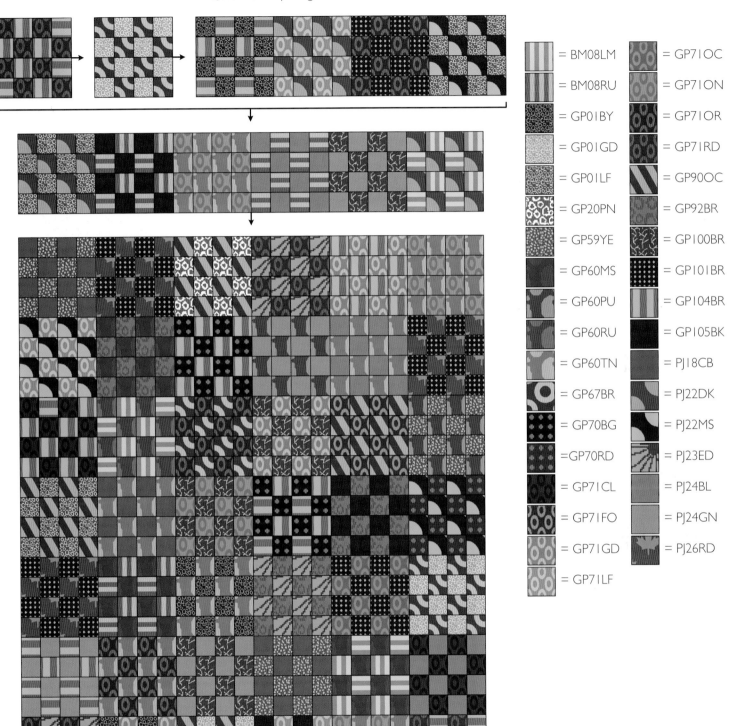

= BM08LM   = GP71OC
= BM08RU   = GP71ON
= GP01BY   = GP71OR
= GP01GD   = GP71RD
= GP01LF   = GP90OC
= GP20PN   = GP92BR
= GP59YE   = GP100BR
= GP60MS   = GP101BR
= GP60PU   = GP104BR
= GP60RU   = GP105BK
= GP60TN   = PJ18CB
= GP67BR   = PJ22DK
= GP70BG   = PJ22MS
=GP70RD   = PJ23ED
= GP71CL   = PJ24BL
= GP71FO   = PJ24GN
= GP71GD   = PJ26RD
= GP71LF

Lightning Quilt ★★★

KAFFE FASSETT

A gorgeous oriental desk with marquetry flower panels gave me the idea for this quilt. I am very excited about finding a new form for a quilt that feels quite traditional but comes from a different world. If I started again I'd try to get all brown marquetry toned fabrics to play with or do another colouring altogether, like dark blues and purples with black sashing.

SIZE OF QUILT
The finished quilt will measure approx.
82½in x 96in (209.5cm x 244cm).

MATERIALS
Patchwork and Border Fabrics:
LOTUS LEAF
Umber   GP29UM: ⅞yd (80cm)
BEKAH
Plum   GP69PL: 1yd (90cm)
ASIAN CIRCLES
Orange   GP89OR: 3¾yds (3.4m)
BUBBLE FLOWER
Dusk   GP97DU: ⅝yd (60cm)
Teal   GP97TE: ⅝yd (60cm)
WOOD EAR
Red   GP99RD: ¾yd (70cm)
GLORY ROSE
Red   PJ21RD: ¾yd (70cm)
WALTZING MATILDA
Dark   PJ22DK: ⅞yd (80cm)
DELPHINIUM
Red   PJ25RD: ⅝yd (60cm)
LAYERED LEAVES
Red   PJ26RD: 1¾yds (1.6m)
Rust   PJ26RU: ⅞yd (80cm)

Backing Fabric: 6⅞yds (6.3m)
We suggest these fabrics for backing:
WOOD EAR Red, GP99RD
LOTUS LEAF Umber, GP29UM
WALTZING MATILDA Dark, PJ22DK

Binding:
MIRAGE STRIPE
Brown   GP104BR: ⅞yd (80cm)

Batting:
90in x 104in (228.5cm x 264cm).

Quilting Thread:
Toning machine quilting thread.

Templates:

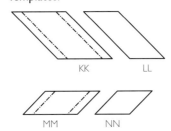

KK   LL

MM   NN

PATCH SHAPES
The centre of this quilt is made up using 2 parallelogram shapes (Templates LL and NN), which are interspaced with narrow sashing strips. We have also provided 2 further parallelogram templates (Templates KK and MM) which incorporate the sashing strips as it is much easier to piece the fabric and then cut the shapes. The parallelograms are pieced into straight set rows, alternating across the width with template KK (pieced with sashing) and LL (not pieced) for the wide rows and template MM (pieced with sashing) and NN (not pieced) for the narrow rows. The row ends are pieced oversized and then trimmed once the quilt centre is complete. The quilt centre is then surrounded with a pieced border. The templates for this quilt are printed at 50% of true size, photocopy at 200% before using.

CUTTING OUT
The following fabrics are pieced into strip sets with GP89OR sashing fabric and used for pieced parallelograms (Templates KK and MM): GP69PL, GP97DU, GP97TE, PJ21RD and PJ22DK. The remaining fabrics are not pre–pieced.
Template KK (pieced parallelograms): For each strip set cut one 4in (10.25cm) strip across the width of the main fabric and two 1½in (3.75cm) strips across the width of the fabric in GP89OR. Each pieced strip will give you 3 patches per full width. Stitch a GP89OR strip to each side of the main fabric strip to make a complete strip set. Cut 15 parallelograms in GP69PL, 13 in PJ22DK, 12 in PJ21RD, 9 in GP97DU and GP97TE.
Template MM (pieced parallelograms): For each strip set cut one 4in (10.25cm) strip across the width of the main fabric and two 1½in (3.75cm) strips across the width of the fabric in GP89OR. Each pieced strip will give you 6 patches per full width. Stitch a GP89OR strip to each side of the main fabric strip to make a complete strip set. Cut 13 parallelograms in GP69PL, 11 in PJ22DK, 10 in PJ21RD, 8 in GP97DU and GP97TE.
Template LL: Cut 4in (10.25cm) strips across the width of the fabric. Each strip will give you 3 patches per full width. Cut 14 in GP29UM, PJ26RU, 11 in GP99RD, 10 in PJ25RD and 9 in PJ26RD.
Template NN: Cut 4in (10.25cm) strips across the width of the fabric. Each strip will give you 6 patches per full width. Cut 12 in GP29UM, PJ26RU, 9 in GP99RD, 8 in PJ25RD and PJ26RD.

Borders: Cut 9 strips 4in (10.25cm) wide in PJ26RD, join as necessary and cut 2 border strips 85½in (217.25cm) long for the quilt sides and 2 border strips 83in (210.75cm) long for the quilt top and bottom. Cut 17 strips 1½in (3.75cm) wide in GP89OR. Join as necessary and add a strip to each side of each border strip.

Binding: Cut 10 strips 2½in (6.5cm) wide across the width of the fabric in GP104BR.

Backing: Cut 2 pieces 40in x 104in (101.5cm

Row Assembly Diagrams

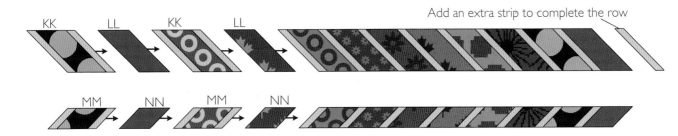

Add an extra strip to complete the row

KK   LL   KK   LL

MM   NN   MM   NN

x 264cm) 2 pieces 40in x 11in (101.5cm x 28cm) and 1 piece 11in x 25in (28cm x 63.5cm) in backing fabric.

MAKING THE QUILT

Use a ¼in (6mm) seam allowance throughout. Referring to the quilt assembly diagram for fabric placement lay out the parallelograms in 17 rows as shown in the row assembly diagram, alternating the pieced and plain across the width. On the top row, 8th and 9th rows add a scrap of GP89OR

fabric to the right side of the row so that when the quilt side is trimmed the row will be complete. This is not necessary on other rows. Join the rows to complete the quilt centre. Trim the sides of the quilt centre as shown in the trimming diagram leaving a ¼in (6mm) seam allowance OUTSIDE the drawn line. The trimmed quilt is shown in the quilt assembly diagram.

ADDING THE BORDERS

Add the side borders then the top and

bottom borders as shown in the quilt assembly diagram to complete the quilt.

FINISHING THE QUILT

Press the quilt top. Seam the backing pieces using a ¼in (6mm) seam allowance to form a piece approx 90in x 104in (228.5cm x 264cm). Layer the quilt top, batting and backing and baste together (see page 139). Using toning machine quilting thread, quilt in the ditch along the sashing seams to highlight the lightning pattern. Quilt the border in the same way. Trim the quilt edges and attach the binding (see page 140).

Trimming Diagram

= GP29UM

= GP69PL

= GP89OR

= GP97DU

= GP97TE

= GP99RD

= PJ21RD

= PJ22DK

= PJ25RD

= PJ26RD

= PJ26RU

Quilt Assembly Diagram

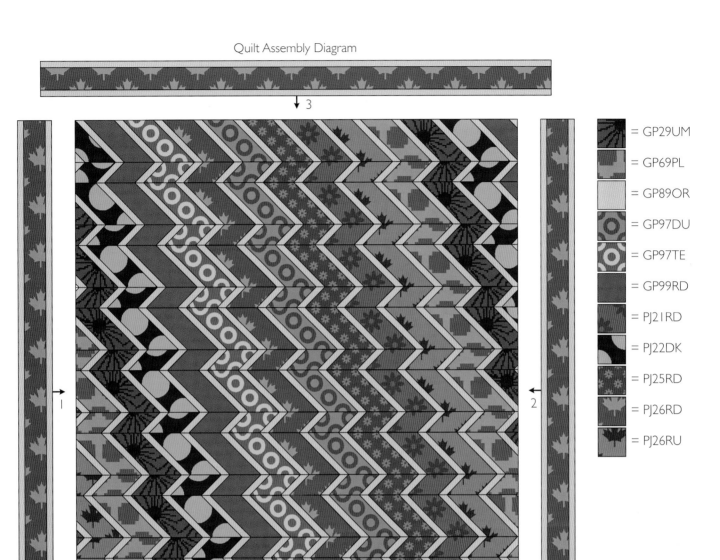

= GP29UM

= GP69PL

= GP89OR

= GP97DU

= GP97TE

= GP99RD

= PJ21RD

= PJ22DK

= PJ25RD

= PJ26RD

= PJ26RU

Fruit Salad Quilt ★★

LIZA PRIOR LUCY

This is a scrappy quilt. It isn't necessary to place each fabric as in the original. Sprinkle the pieced triangles throughout and keep the dark colours pointing up and the light colours pointing down and the design will work out just fine.

SIZE OF QUILT
The finished quilt will measure approx.
83in × 93in (211cm × 236.5cm).

MATERIALS
We have drawn the quilt showing the exact placement Liza used, however this is meant to be a 'scrappy style' quilt and exact placement of fabrics are not important.

Patchwork and Border Fabrics:

LIGHT FABRICS:
ZINNIA
Pink   GP31PK: ½yd (45cm)
SPOT
Peach   GP70PH: ⅛yd (15cm)
ABORIGINAL DOTS
Lime   GP71LM: ⅛yd (15cm)
ASIAN CIRCLES
Yellow   GP89YE: ⅜yd (35cm)
BIG BLOOMS
Pink   GP91PK: ⅜yd (35cm)
LAKE BLOSSOMS
Yellow   GP93YE: ⅜yd (35cm)
HENNA
Yellow   GP96YE: ⅜yd (35cm)
BUBBLE FLOWER
Summer   GP97SU: ⅜yd (35cm)
KIRMAN
Orange   GP98OR: 3¾yds (3.4m)
                        (incl. Borders)

GARDEN PARTY
Yellow   PJ20YE: ⅜yd (35cm)
GLORY ROSE
Yellow   PJ21YE: ⅜yd (35cm)
TROPICAL
Pink   PJ23PK: ⅜yd (35cm)
COLEUS
Yellow   PJ30YE: ¼yd (25cm)
SHOT COTTON
Sunshine   SC35: ⅛yd (15cm)
Apple   SC39: ⅛yd (15cm)

DARK FABRICS:
ROMAN GLASS
Red   GP01RD: ¼yd (25cm)
ZINNIA
Lime   GP31LM: ⅜yd (35cm)
CLOISONNE
Magenta   GP46MG: ⅜yd (35cm)
GUINEA FLOWER
Apricot   GP59AP: ⅜yd (35cm)
SPOT
Fuchsia   GP70FU: ⅛yd (15cm)
ASIAN CIRCLES
Tomato   GP89TM: ⅝yd (60cm)
BIG BLOOMS
Red   GP91RD: ⅜yd (35cm)
LAKE BLOSSOMS
Red   GP93RD: ⅝yd (60cm)
BUBBLE FLOWER
Magenta   GP97MG: ⅜yd (35cm)
KIRMAN
Red   GP98RD: ½yd (45cm)
PERSIAN VASE
Red   GP100RD: ¼yd (25cm)
GARDEN PARTY
Coral   PJ20CO: ⅜yd (35cm)
SHOT COTTON
Watermelon   SC33: ⅛yd (15cm)

Backing Fabric: 8⅛yds (7.4m)
We suggest these fabrics for backing:
ASIAN CIRCLES Tomato, GP89TM
BUBBLE FLOWER Summer, GP97SU
GARDEN PARTY Yellow, PJ20YE

Binding:
DIAGONAL STRIPE
Pink   GP90PK: ¾yd (70cm)

Batting:
91in × 101in (231cm × 256.5cm).

Quilting Thread:
Orange machine quilting thread.

Templates:

K   L   M & Reverse M

PATCH SHAPES
The centre of this quilt is pieced using 2 sizes of equilateral triangle patch shapes. The smaller triangles (Template L) are pieced to form large triangles, the same size as the large triangles (Template K). These are pieced into straight set rows, the ends of which are filled using a right angled triangle patch shape (Template M and Reverse M). The quilt centre is then surrounded with a border with corner posts. The border is pieced to make best use of the KIRMAN fabric design.

CUTTING OUT
We have specified the exact number of patches to cut in each fabric to make Liza's quilt as shown, however it is not critical to follow the quantities exactly, if you like a particular fabric, then add more of that and reduce another. You can also vary the number and position of the pieced triangles as you wish. Also, some fabrics have light and dark areas in the design so may be used in either group. Cut the borders first and use leftover fabric for templates.

Borders: The KIRMAN fabric design (GP98OR) is directional and has a distinct bouquet of flowers that is centred in all the borders, refer to the photograph for details. Cut 1 layer of fabric at a time. The top and bottom borders must be pieced with the

Block Assembly Diagrams

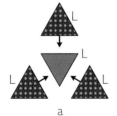

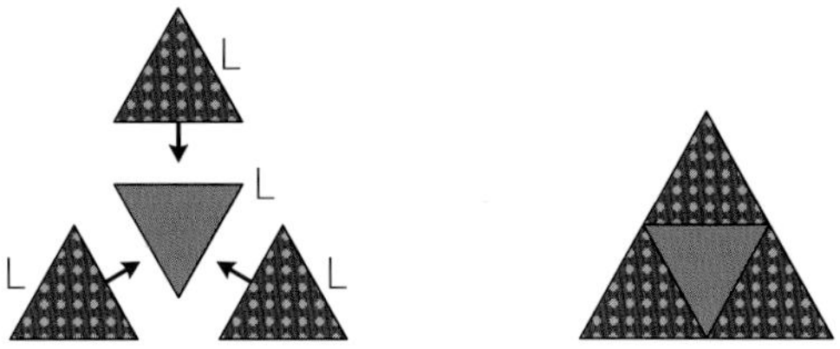

a

b

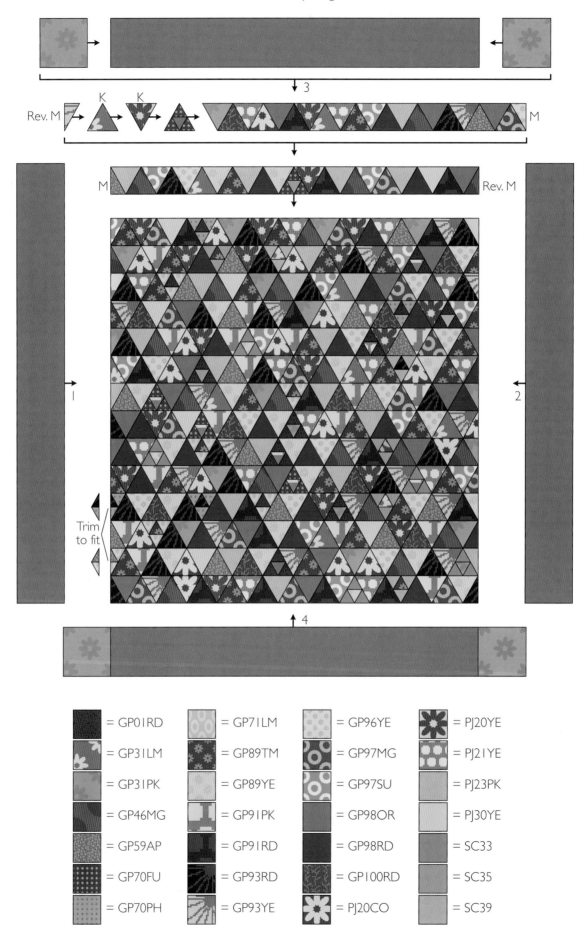

= GP01RD	= GP71LM	= GP96YE	= PJ20YE
= GP31LM	= GP89TM	= GP97MG	= PJ21YE
= GP31PK	= GP89YE	= GP97SU	= PJ23PK
= GP46MG	= GP91PK	= GP98OR	= PJ30YE
= GP59AP	= GP91RD	= GP98RD	= SC33
= GP70FU	= GP91RD	= GP100RD	= SC35
= GP70PH	= GP93YE	= PJ20CO	= SC39

floral pattern matched up at the seams. Open the fabric and press well. Find the largest flowers in the vase and mark the centre of that bouquet with a pin or chalk. Keeping that in the centre cut a panel 12in (30.5cm) wide from selvedge to selvedge. For the next 3 cuts it isn't necessary to find the centre flowers, just cut 3 more 12in (30.5cm) panels. Sew these 4 panels end to end, matching the fabric pattern. Mark the centre flower bouquet and trim to 8½in (21.5cm) wide centring on the bouquet. The top and bottom borders are cut from this long length. Make sure a bouquet is in the centre of both the top and bottom borders. Cut 2 strips 8½in x 66⅜in (21.5cm x 168.5cm).

For the side borders, cut 2 strips 8½in x 76½in (21.5cm x 194.25cm) down the length of the fabric making sure a bouquet is in the centre of each border.

Border Corner Posts: Cut 4 8½in (21.5cm) squares in GP31PK.

Template K: Cut 5½in (14cm) strips across the width of the fabric. Each strip will give you 11 patches per full width. Cut 24 in GP89TM, 23 in GP93RD, 22 in GP98RD, 19 in GP46MG, PJ20YE, PJ23PK, 18 in GP89YE, 17 in GP91PK, GP93YE, GP98OR, PJ20CO, 16 in GP91RD, PJ21YE, 15 in GP59AP, 14 in GP96YE, GP97MG, 12 in GP31PK, GP97SU, 10 in GP100RD, 8 in GP31LM and 7 in PJ30YE. Total 336 Triangles. Reserve leftover strips for other templates.

Template M and reverse M: From leftover strips cut 2 in GP31PK, GP59AP, GP89TM, GP93RD, 1 in GP31LM, GP46MG, GP89YE, GP93YE, GP96YE, GP98OR, PJ23PK and PJ30YE. Total 16 triangles. Reverse the template by turning it over and cut 2 in GP89TM, GP98RD, 1 in GP31PK, GP46MG, GP91PK, GP93RD, GP93YE, GP97MG, GP97SU, GP98OR, PJ20CO and PJ23PK. Total 14 triangles.

Template L: Cut 3⅛in (8cm) strips across the width of the fabric. Each strip will give you 21 patches per full width. Cut 26 in GP01RD, 17 in GP71LM, 15 in GP70FU, SC33, 11 in GP70PH, SC35, 10 in SC39, 6 in GP91PK, 5 in GP89TM, 3 in GP31PK, GP93RD, 2 in GP31LM, GP89YE, GP98OR, GP98RD, 1 in GP59AP, GP96YE, GP97MG and PJ21YE. Total 134 triangles.

Binding: Cut 9 strips 2½in (6.5cm) wide across the width of the fabric in GP90PK.

Backing: Cut 2 pieces 40in x 91in (101.5cm x 231cm) and 1 piece 22in x 91in (56cm x 231cm) in backing fabric.

MAKING THE QUILT

Use a ¼in (6mm) seam allowance throughout and refer to the quilt assembly diagram for fabric placement. This is a scrappy style quilt, it isn't necessary to place each fabric as in the original to achieve the same effect, the only rule is that the light fabric triangles point down and the dark fabric triangles point up. Piece a total of 32 blocks following block assembly diagram a, the finished block can be seen in diagram b. Also piece 2 partial blocks each using 3 template L triangles, these will be used along the side of the quilt and trimmed to fit.

Lay out the pieced blocks and template K triangles into 16 rows as shown in the quilt assembly diagram. Complete the row ends with the template M and reverse M triangles and partial blocks. Piece the rows and then join the rows to form the quilt centre. Trim the partial blocks to fit and then add the side borders to the quilt centre as shown in the quilt assembly diagram, ensuring that the design is the right way up. Add a corner post to each end of the top and bottom borders and add to the quilt centre to complete the quilt, again ensuring the design is the right way up.

FINISHING THE QUILT

Press the quilt top. Seam the backing pieces using a ¼in (6mm) seam allowance to form a piece approx. 91in x 101in (231cm x 256.5cm). Layer the quilt top, batting and backing and baste together (see page 139). Using orange thread free motion quilt throughout, following the images in the fabric patterns, making the flowers pop and giving an embossed appearance. Trim the quilt edges and attach the binding (see page 140).

Mexican Party Quilt ★★★

KAFFE FASSETT

I popped open a book on Indian patchwork and spotted this jolly patchwork lay out. I loved the jaunty mood created by simple squares on point. The large squares show off the upscale floral prints a treat.

SIZE OF QUILT
The finished quilt will measure approx.
76in × 76in (193cm × 193cm).

MATERIALS
Patchwork Fabrics:
WAVES
Lipstick	BM04LP: ½yd (45cm)

DAPPLE
Blue	BM05BL: ¼yd (25cm)
Pink	BM05PK: ⅜yd (35cm)
Red	BM05RD: ⅝yd (60cm)
Yellow	BM05YE: ¼yd (25cm)

GUINEA FLOWER
Apricot	GP59AP: ¼yd (25cm)
Pink	GP59PK: ⅝yd (60cm)

SPOT
Fuchsia	GP70FU: ½yd (45cm)
Gold	GP70GD: ⅝yd (60cm)
Turquoise	GP70TQ: ½yd (45cm)

ABORIGINAL DOTS
Orange	GP71OR: ½yd (45cm)
Sweet Pea	GP71SW: 2⅛yds (2m)

RUSSIAN ROSE
Pastel	GP95PT: ⅜yd (35cm)
Yellow	GP95YE: ⅜yd (35cm)

BUBBLE FLOWER
Magenta	GP97MG: ⅜yd (35cm)

KIRMAN
Duck Egg	GP98DE: ⅜yd (35cm)

GARDEN PARTY
Yellow	PJ20YE: ⅜yd (35cm)

GLORY ROSE
Magenta	PJ21MG: ⅜yd (35cm)

TROPICAL
Pink	PJ23PK: ⅜yd (35cm)

LAYERED LEAVES
Yellow	PJ26YE: ⅜yd (35cm)

Backing Fabric: 5½yds (5m)
We suggest these fabrics for backing:
GLORY ROSE Magenta, PJ21MG
DAPPLE Blue, BM05BL

Binding:
DAPPLE
Yellow	BM05YE: ⅝yd (60cm)

Batting:
84in × 84in (213.5cm × 213.5cm).

Quilting Thread:
Toning machine quilting thread.

Templates:

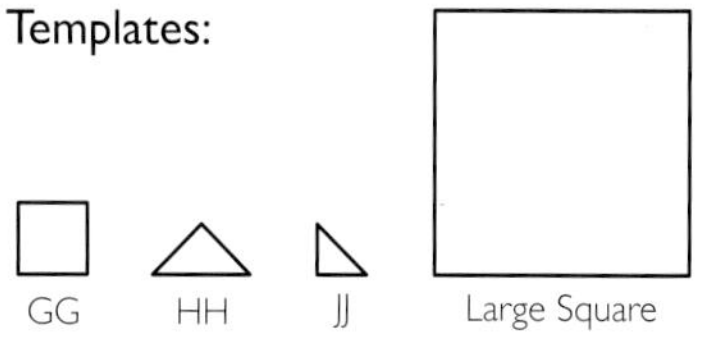

GG   HH   JJ   Large Square

PATCH SHAPES
The floral squares in this quilt (Large Square, cut to size) are fussy cut to generally centre on the blooms in the fabric designs. Each square is then surrounded, 'courthouse steps' style with inner and outer framing strips (cut to size). The framed blocks are then interspaced with pieced sashing strips which use 1 square patch shape (Template GG) and 2 triangle patch shapes (Template HH and JJ) and pieced sashing posts which use the same square patch shape (Template GG) and one of the triangle patch shapes (Template JJ).

CUTTING OUT
The template GG, HH and JJ shapes used in the quilt are not standard sizes. The strip sizes we quote are very slightly larger than necessary. We strongly recommend that you make plastic or card templates and cut the

Block Assembly Diagrams

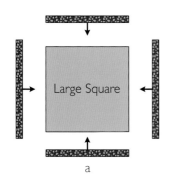

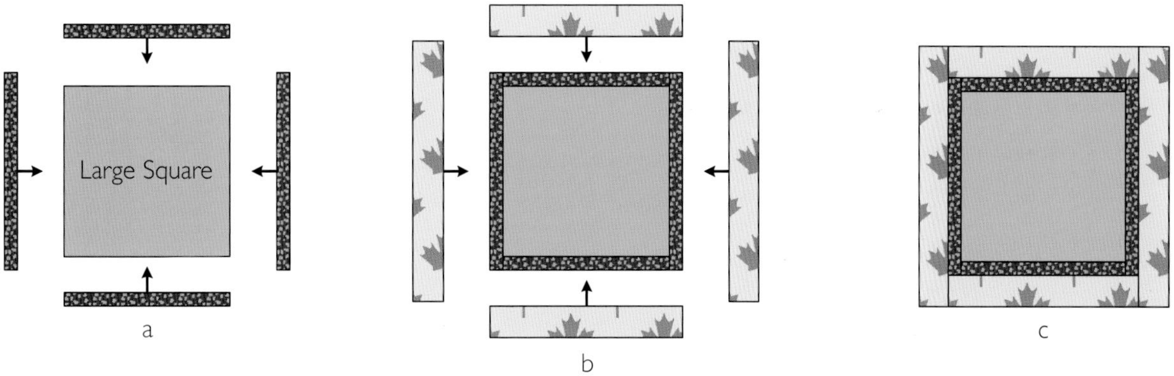

a

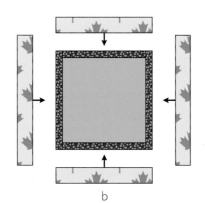

b

c

final shapes using these. Cut the fabric in the order stated to prevent waste.

Large Squares: Cut 10in × 10in (25.5cm × 25.5cm) squares centring on the floral blooms. Cut 3 in GP95YE, GP98DE, PJ21MG, PJ23PK, 2 in GP95PT and PJ20YE.

Inner Framing Strips: 1 set of inner framing strips consists of 2 strips 1¼in × 10in (3.25cm × 25.5cm) and 2 strips 1¼in × 11½in (3.25cm × 29.25cm). Cut strips 1¼in (3.25cm) wide across the width of the fabric, you will need 2 strips for 1 set of inner framing strips or 3 strips for 2 sets.
Cut 2 sets in BM05RD, GP59PK, GP70GD, GP70TQ, GP97MG, 1 set in BM04LP, BM05PK, GP59AP, GP70FU, GP71OR and PJ26YE.

Outer Framing Strips: 1 set of outer framing strips consists of 2 strips 2¼in × 11½in (5.75cm × 29.25cm) and 2 strips 2¼in × 15in (5.75cm × 38cm). Cut strips 2¼in (5.75cm) wide across the width of the fabric, you will need 2 strips for 1 set of inner framing strips or 3 strips for 2 sets. To get 2 sets from 3 strips careful cutting is required. From the 1st and 2nd strip cut 1 long (15in/38cm) strip and 2 short (11½in/29.25cm) outer framing strips, from the 3rd strip cut 2 long (15in/38cm) outer framing strips.
Cut 2 sets in BM05PK, BM05RD, BM05YE, GP59PK, GP70GD, PJ26YE, 1 set in BM04LP, GP70FU, GP70TQ and GP71OR.

Template GG: Cut 3⅛in (8cm) strips across the width of the fabric. Each strip will give you 12 patches per full width. Cut 24 in GP70TQ, 23 in GP70GD, 20 in BM04LP, GP70FU, GP97MG, 18 in BM05BL, GP71OR, 16 in BM05RD, GP59PK and 10 in GP59AP.

Template HH: Cut 4⅞in (12.5cm) strips across the width of the fabric. Each strip will give you 32 patches per full width. From the strips cut 4⅞in (12.5cm) squares, then cut each square twice diagonally to make 4 triangles, trim to the exact size using the template. This will ensure the long side of the triangle will not have a bias edge. Note: do not move the patches until both diagonals have been cut. Cut 240 triangles in GP71SW.

Template JJ: Cut 2¾in (7cm) strips across the width of the fabric. Each strip will give you 28 patches per full width, trim to the exact size using the template. Cut 260 in GP71SW.

Binding: Cut 8 strips 2½in (6.5cm) wide across the width of the fabric in BM05YE.

Backing: Cut 2 pieces 40in × 84in (101.5cm × 213.5cm) 2 pieces 40in × 5in (101.5cm × 12.75cm) and 1 piece 5in × 5in (12.75cm × 12.75cm) in backing fabric.

MAKING THE BLOCKS
Use a ¼in (6mm) seam allowance throughout and refer to the quilt assembly diagram for fabric placement. Take the large squares and add inner, then outer framing strips as shown in block assembly diagrams a and b, the framed block can be seen in diagram c, make 16.

MAKING THE PIECED SASHING
Make up 40 pieced sashing strips as shown in block assembly diagram d, the finished pieced sashing strip can be seen in diagram e. Make up 25 pieced sashing posts as shown in diagram f, the finished pieced sashing post can be seen in diagram g.

MAKING THE QUILT
Lay out the framed blocks interspaced with the pieced sashing strips and pieced sashing posts, Piece into 9 rows as shown in the quilt assembly diagram. Join the rows to complete the quilt.

FINISHING THE QUILT
Press the quilt top. Seam the backing pieces using a ¼in (6mm) seam allowance to form a piece approx. 84in × 84in (213.5cm × 213.5cm). Layer the quilt top, batting and backing and baste together (see page 139). Using toning machine quilting thread quilt all the framing and sashing seams in the ditch. Free motion meander quilt following the fabric designs in the template large squares. Trim the quilt edges and attach the binding (see page 140).

Block Assembly Diagrams

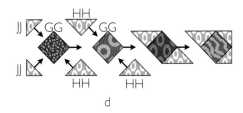

d

e

f

g

Quilt Assembly Diagram

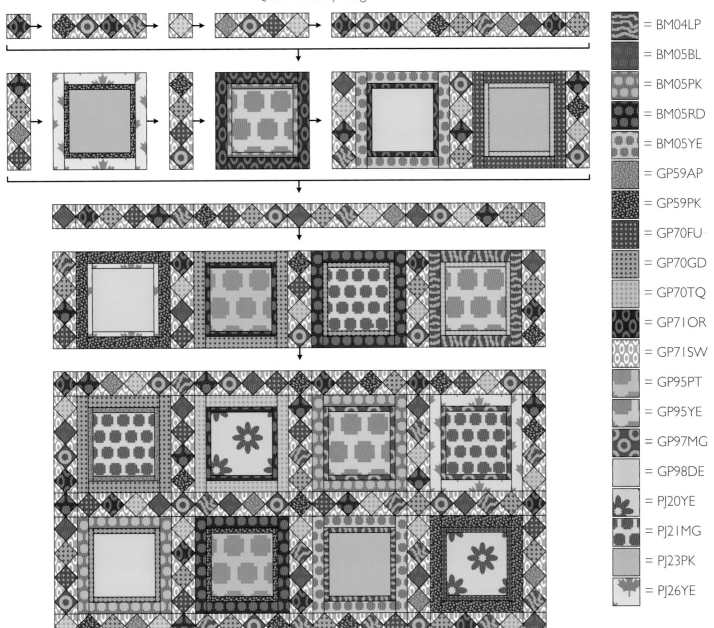

= BM04LP
= BM05BL
= BM05PK
= BM05RD
= BM05YE
= GP59AP
= GP59PK
= GP70FU
= GP70GD
= GP70TQ
= GP71OR
= GP71SW
= GP95PT
= GP95YE
= GP97MG
= GP98DE
= PJ20YE
= PJ21MG
= PJ23PK
= PJ26YE

Blush Quilt ★

PAULINE SMITH

I began with a very different quilt in mind but as I sifted through the fabrics and thinking of Roussillon as our location, I began picking out closely toned red and pink prints. I quickly abandoned plan A and decided to try this simple layout which relies on close tones to work successfully. I'm very pleased with the result.

SIZE OF QUILT
The finished quilt will measure approx.
87½in x 87½in (222.25cm x 222.25cm).

MATERIALS
Patchwork Fabrics:

WAVES
Lipstick   BM04LP: ⅜yd (35cm)

ROMAN GLASS
Pink   GP01PK: ¾yd (70cm)

ZINNIA
Pink   GP31PK: 1¼yds (1.15m)

GUINEA FLOWER
Apricot   GP59AP: 1¼yds (1.15m)

SPOT
Fuchsia   GP70FU: 1yd (90cm)

ASIAN CIRCLES
Tomato   GP89TM: ⅞yd (80cm)

BIG BLOOMS
Red   GP91RD: ¼yd (25cm)

BUBBLE FLOWER
Magenta   GP97MG: ¾yd (70cm)
Summer   GP97SU: 1yd (90cm)

KIRMAN
Red   GP98RD: ½yd (45cm)

GLORY ROSE
Pink   PJ21PK: ½yd (45cm)

LAYERED LEAVES
Celadon   PJ26CD: ½yd (45cm)

Backing Fabric: 7yds (6.4m)
We suggest these fabrics for backing:
GLORY ROSE Pink, PJ21PK
SPOT Fuchsia, GP70FU

Binding:
ASIAN CIRCLES
Tomato   GP89TM: ¾yd (70cm)

Batting:
95in × 95in (241.5cm × 241.5cm).

Quilting Thread:
Toning machine quilting thread.

Templates:

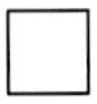

E

PATCH SHAPES
This quilt is pieced using a single square patch shape (Template E), the squares are set in simple rows, ideal for a beginner.

CUTTING OUT
Template E: Cut 4in (10.25cm) strips across the width of the fabric. Each strip will give you 10 patches per full width. Cut 97 in GP31PK, 92 in GP59AP, 80 in GP70FU, 72 in GP97SU, 64 in GP89TM, 56 in GP01PK, 48 in GP97MG, 40 in PJ26CD, 32 in GP98RD, 24 in PJ21PK, 16 in BM04LP and 4 in GP91RD.

Binding: Cut 9 strips 2½in (6.5cm) wide across the width of the fabric in GP89TM.

Backing: Cut 2 pieces 40in × 95in (101.5cm × 241.5cm), 2 pieces 40in × 16in (101.5cm × 40.5cm) and 1 piece 16in × 16in (40.5cm × 40.5cm) in backing fabric. Note: For a quirky look to the backing you could cut the 16in (40.5cm) square from a different fabric and piece the backing with the contrasting square in the centre.

MAKING THE QUILT
Use a ¼in (6mm) seam allowance throughout. Arrange the squares as shown in the quilt assembly diagram, we recommend using a design wall or laying the blocks out on the floor to check the layout. Join the squares into 25 rows of 25 squares and then join the rows to complete the quilt.

FINISHING THE QUILT
Press the quilt top. Seam the backing pieces using a ¼in (6mm) seam allowance to form a piece approx. 95in × 95in (241.5cm × 241.5cm). Layer the quilt top, batting and backing and baste together (see page 139). Using toning thread machine quilt in the ditch in all the seams. Trim the quilt edges and attach the binding (see page 140).

Quilt Assembly Diagram

= BM04LP

= GP01PK

= GP31PK

= GP59AP

= GP70FU

= GP89TM

= GP91RD

= GP97MG

= GP97SU

= GP98RD

= PJ21PK

= PJ26CD

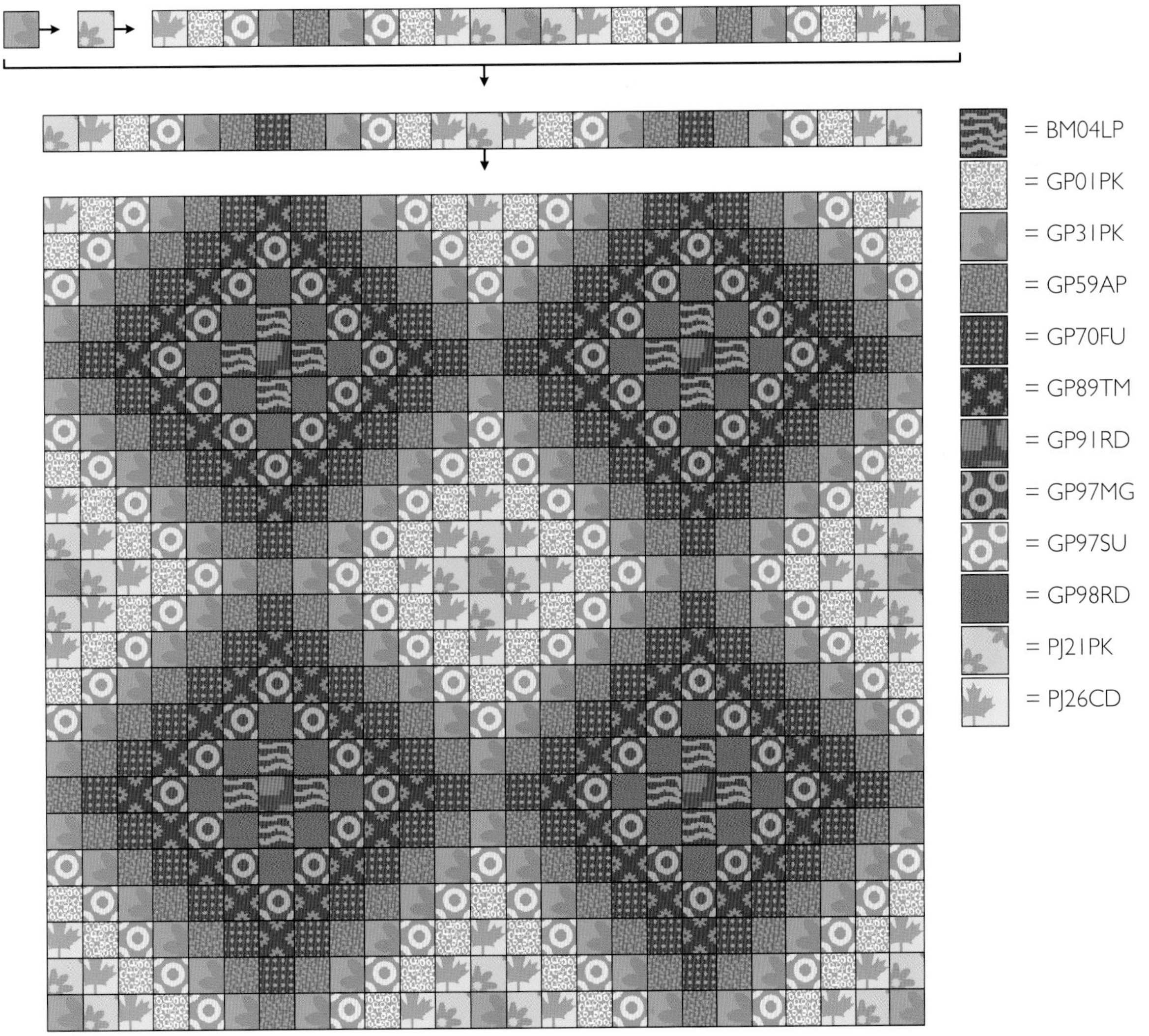

Cheerful Party Quilt ★★
MARY MASHUTA

Whether inside or outdoors, this quilt will cheer up any party.

SIZE OF QUILT
The finished quilt will measure approx.
78in x 78in (198cm x 198cm).

MATERIALS
Patchwork Fabrics:
WAVES
Circus	BM04CR: ⅞yd (80cm
Lipstick	BM04LP: 1⅝yds (1.5m)
DAPPLE	
Yellow	BM05YE: 1⅝yds (1.5m)
FISHLIPS	
Pastel	BM07PT: ⅝yd (60cm)
ROMAN GLASS	
Leafy	GP01LF: ½yd (45cm)
Red	GP01RD: ¼yd (25cm)
SPOT	
Yellow	GP70YE: 1⅝yds (1.5m)
GARDEN PARTY	
Yellow	PJ20YE: 2yds (1.8m)

Backing Fabric: 5⅞yds (5.4m)
We suggest these fabrics for backing:
GLORY ROSE Magenta, PJ21MG
DAPPLE Yellow, BM05YE
SPOT Yellow, GP70YE

Binding:
ROMAN GLASS
Red   GP01RD: ¾yd (70cm)

Batting:
86in x 86in (218.5cm x 218.5cm).

Quilting Thread:
Toning and yellow machine quilting thread.

Templates:

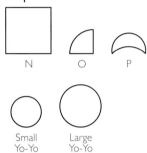

This quilt also uses a card circle template
which is on page 129.
Note: Use card for making template P as it

will be trimmed and used for pressing during
the quilt construction.

PATCH SHAPES
The background for the Party blocks, which
finish to 12in (30.5cm) square, are pieced
using a square patch shape (Template N).
Each block has an appliquéd centre, made
with a quarter circle patch shape (Template
O) and a petal patch shape (Template P) and
a set of 2 layered Yo–Yos in the centre. The
blocks are interspaced with sashing and
corner posts, (cut to size). The quilt is finished
with a simple border with corner posts (cut
to size).

CUTTING OUT
Important Information:
Please read carefully before cutting the
WAVES stripe fabric used for petals
(BM04CR) and sashing (BM04LP).
Open out the fabric and cut 1 layer at a time
A gridded ruler helps to get the first accurate
cut across the stripe even though this is a
wavy stripe.
Keep checking as you go that the cuts are at

Block Assembly Diagrams

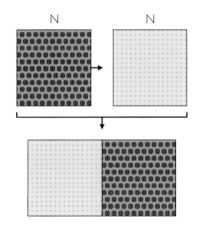

a

b

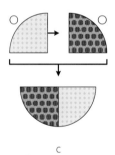

c

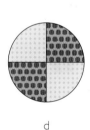

d

e

f

90 degrees to the stripe direction and take time to correct if necessary. The final appearance is worth it.

Template N: Cut 6½in (16.5cm) strips across the width of the fabric. Each strip will give you 6 patches per full width. Cut 32 in BM05YE and GP70YE.
Template O: Cut 3⅝in (9.25cm) strips across the width of the fabric. Each strip will give you 11 patches per full width. Cut 32 in BM05YE and GP70YE.
Template P: Cut 3¼in (8.25cm) strips across the width of the fabric. Each strip will give you 8 patches per full width. Cut 64 in BM04CR.
Large Yo–Yo: Cut 16 circles in GP01LF.
Small Yo–Yo: Cut 16 circles in GP01RD.
Sashing Strips: Cut 3½in (9cm) strips across the width of the fabric. Each strip will give you 3 patches per full width. Cut 40 strips 3½in x 12½in (9cm x 31.75cm) in BM04LP.
Border Corner Posts: Cut 4 squares 8in x 8in (20.25cm x 20.25cm) in BM07PT.
Sashing Corner Posts: Cut 3½in (9cm) strips across the width of the fabric. Each strip will give you 3 patches per full width. Cut 25 squares 3½in x 3½in (9cm x 9cm) in BM07PT.
Borders: Cut 4 strips down the length of the fabric 8in x 63½in (20.25cm x 161.25cm) in PJ20YE.

Binding: Cut 9 strips 2½in (6.5cm) wide across the width of the fabric in GP01RD.

Backing: Cut 2 pieces 40in x 86in (101.5cm x 218.5cm), 2 pieces 40in x 7in (101.5cm x 17.75cm) and 1 piece 7in x 7in (17.75cm x 17.75cm) in backing fabric. Note: For a quirky look to the backing you could cut the 7in (17.75cm) square from a different fabric and piece the backing with the contrasting square in the centre.

MAKING THE BLOCKS
Use a ¼in (6mm) seam allowance throughout. Refer to the quilt assembly diagram for fabric placement. Piece 16 block backgrounds as shown in block assembly diagrams a and b. Make the circle card template printed on page 129, use thin card as this will be used to gather the fabric over and form smooth curved edges to the appliqué shapes. Join 4 template O quarter circles to form a circle as shown in diagrams c and d. Work a running stitch with strong thread ⅛in (3mm) from the outer edge of the pieced circle, overlap the first and last

stitches. Place the card circle in the centre of the wrong side of the pieced circle and pull up the gathering stitches over the card. Press with the card in place then remove the card. This makes the centre of the appliqué shape. Make 16.

Take the card template P and carefully remove the seam allowance from the outside curved edge ONLY. Take a template P fabric petal and work a running stitch with strong thread ⅛in (3mm) in from the outer curve only. Place the fabric petal over the card petal, pull up the gathering stitches to form an even curve, press carefully and remove the card. Repeat until you have 4 petals for each circle.

Hand baste the 4 petals to the pieced circle, matching the dots and seam allowances on the wrong side, as shown in diagram e. Carefully place the completed flower onto a block background as shown in diagram f. Stitch the centre, then the petals to the background block. This can be done by hand or machine using a blanket, straight or invisible stitch. Turn the block over and cut

away excess fabric from behind the appliquéd flower leaving a ¼in (6mm) seam allowance. Make 16.

MAKING THE YO–YOS
Turn under a ¼in (6mm) hem around each fabric circle and sew a running stitch using strong thread around the outer edge, overlapping the first and last stitches. Making sure the right side of the fabric is the outside of the Yo–Yo, gently pull the thread, gathering the fabric until a very small opening is left. Knot the thread and flatten the Yo–Yo manipulating the fabric until a regular circle is produced. Make 16 large and 16 small Yo–Yos. Put to one side until after the quilting is complete.

MAKING THE QUILT
Join the blocks and sashing into rows as indicated in the quilt assembly diagram, join the rows to form the quilt centre. Add the side borders to the quilt centre as shown in the quilt assembly diagram. Add a corner post to each end of the top and bottom borders and add to the quilt centre to complete the quilt.

Quilting Diagram

FINISHING THE QUILT

Press the quilt top. Seam the backing pieces using a ¼in (6mm) seam allowance to form a piece approx. 86in × 86in (218.5cm × 218.5cm). Layer the quilt top, batting and backing and baste together (see page 139). Using toning machine quilting thread quilt in the ditch of the sashing and border seams and around the flowers in each block. Using yellow thread quilt the blocks, sashing, borders and corner blocks as shown in the quilting diagram. Trim the quilt edges and attach the binding (see page 140). Finally add a stacked double Yo–Yo (GP01LF on the bottom and GP01RD on the top) to each flower centre.

Quilt Assembly Diagram

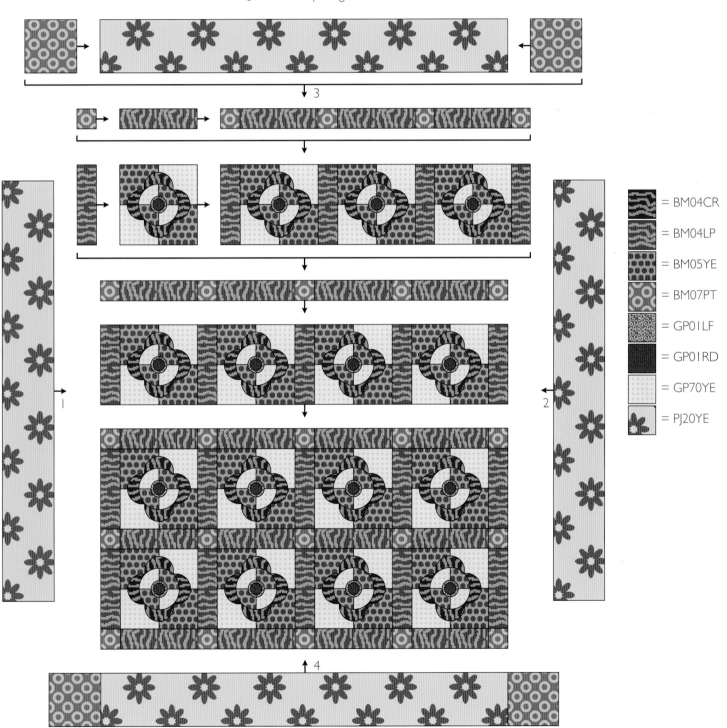

= BM04CR

= BM04LP

= BM05YE

= BM07PT

= GP01LF

= GP01RD

= GP70YE

= PJ20YE

Sashed Boxes Quilt ★★★

Kaffe Fassett

I took this design from a vintage quilt done in hexagons. Thinking of the colours of the warm Roussillon walls I decided on a rich golden palette. I used many small scale dots and stripes and the result really pleases me.

SIZE OF QUILT
The finished quilt will measure approx.
65in × 71in (165cm × 180.25cm).

MATERIALS
Patchwork and Border Fabrics:
TENTS
Black   BM03BK: ¼yd (25cm)
Yellow   BM03YE: ¼yd (25cm)
DAPPLE
Pink   BM05PK: ⅜yd (35cm)
Red   BM05RD: ⅝yd (60cm)
SPOT
Gold   GP70GD: ⅞yd (80cm)
Ice   GP70IC: ½yd (45cm)
Peach   GP70PH: ¼yd (25cm)
Red   GP70RD: ¼yd (25cm)
Tobacco   GP70TO: ⅜yd (35cm)
ABORIGINAL DOTS
Gold   GP71GD: 2yds (1.8m)
Grey   GP71GY: ⅜yd (35cm)
Ochre   GP71OC: ⅞yds (80cm)
FLOWER DOT
Grey   GP87GY: ½yd (45cm)
CHEVRON STRIPE
Brown   GP90BR: ½yd (45cm)
MILLEFIORE
Orange   GP92OR: ½yd (45cm)
LAYERED LEAVES
Yellow   PJ26YE: ½yd (45cm)

Backing Fabric: 4⅜yds (4m)
We suggest these fabrics for backing:
LAYERED LEAVES Yellow, PJ26YE
TENTS Yellow, BM03YE
ABORIGINAL DOTS Grey, GP71GY

Binding:
SPOT
Red   GP70RD: ⅝yd (60cm)

Batting:
73in × 79in (185.5cm × 200.5cm).

Quilting thread:
Toning machine quilting thread.

Templates:

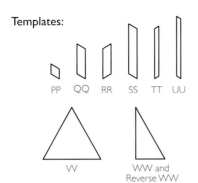

PP QQ RR SS TT UU

VV   WW and
            Reverse WW

PATCH SHAPES
The centre of this quilt is made up pieced
diamonds. These are built in layers around a
diamond patch shape (Template PP). The first
layer uses the same diamond patch shape
(Template PP) and a parallelogram patch
shape (Template QQ). The second layer uses
2 parallelogram patch shapes (Templates RR
and SS). The final layer uses 2 more
parallelogram patch shapes (Templates TT
and UU). The pieced diamonds are pieced in
trios to form hexagon blocks which are
joined to form the quilt centre, along with
extra pieced diamonds and 2 triangle patch
shapes (Templates VV and WW and Reverse
WW) to fill in along the quilt centre edges.
The quilt centre is then surrounded with a
pieced border to complete the quilt.

CUTTING OUT
Cut the fabric in the order stated to prevent
waste. Reserve leftover strips and use for
later templates as appropriate.
Template WW and Reverse WW: Cut 7¼in
(18.5cm) strips across the width of the fabric.
Each strip will give you 18 patches per full
width. Cut 10 in GP71OC, reverse the
template by turning it over and cut 10 in
GP71OC. Reserve the remaining strip and
trim for Template VV.
Template VV: Using the leftover strip from
Template WW and Reverse WW, trim the
strip to 6¾ in (17.25cm) and cut 6 in

GP71OC.
Template PP: Cut 1½in (3.75cm) strips
across the width of the fabric. Each strip will
give you 22 patches per full width. Cut 24 in
GP70IC, 23 in GP71OC, GP87GY, GP92OR,
22 in GP71GY, 20 in PJ26YE, 19 in GP90BR,
18 in GP70TO, 16 in GP70GD, 14 in
BM05RD, 13 in BM05PK, GP70PH, GP70RD,
11 in BM03YE and 9 in BM03BK.
Template QQ: Cut 1½in (3.75cm) strips
across the width of the fabric. Each strip will
give you 9 patches per full width. Cut 18 in
GP70IC, 16 in GP71GY, GP71OC, GP87GY,
14 in GP70TO, GP92OR, 12 in GP70GD,
GP90BR, PJ26YE, 10 in GP70PH, 8 in
BM03YE, BM05RD, GP70RD, 6 in BM05PK
and 4 in BM03BK.
Template RR: Cut 1½in (3.75cm) strips
across the width of the fabric. Each strip will
give you 9 patches per full width. Cut 18 in
GP92OR, 16 in PJ26YE, 14 in BM05PK,
GP71OC, GP87GY, GP90BR, 12 in BM05RD,
GP70IC, GP71GY, 10 in BM03BK, GP70RD, 8 in
GP70GD, GP70TO, 6 in BM03YE and GP70PH.
Template SS: Cut 1½in (3.75cm) strips across
the width of the fabric. Each strip will give
you 6 patches per full width. Cut 18 in
GP92OR, 16 in PJ26YE, 14 in BM05PK,
GP71OC, GP87GY, GP90BR, 12 in BM05RD,
GP70IC, GP71GY, 10 in BM03BK, GP70RD, 8
in GP70GD, GP70TO, 6 in BM03YE and
GP70PH.
Template TT: Cut 1in (2.5cm) strips across
the width of the fabric. Each strip will give
you 6 patches per full width. Cut 174 in
GP71GD.
Template UU: Cut 1in (2.5cm) strips across
the width of the fabric. Each strip will give
you 5 patches per full width. Cut 174 in
GP71GD.
Borders: Cut 7 strips 1½in (3.75cm) wide in
BM05RD, join as necessary and cut 2 border
strips 66⅜in (168.5cm) long for the quilt
sides and 2 border strips 65½in (166.5cm)
long for the quilt top and bottom. Cut 14

strips 1¼in (3.25cm) wide in GP70GD. Join as necessary and add a strip to each side of each border strip.
Binding: Cut 7 strips 2½in (6.5cm) wide across the width of the fabric in GP70RD.
Backing: Cut 2 pieces 40in x 73in (101.5cm x 185.5cm) in backing fabric.

MAKING THE BLOCKS

Use a ¼in (6mm) seam allowance throughout. Referring to the quilt assembly diagram for fabric placement make a total of 87 pieced diamonds as shown in block assembly diagrams a, b and c. The finished diamond can be seen in diagram d. Join the diamonds in trios to form 27 hexagon

blocks as shown in diagram e, using the inset seams method, see the Patchwork Knowhow section, at the back of the book. Reserve the remaining 6 diamonds to fill in the quilt sides.

MAKING THE QUILT

Lay out the hexagon blocks, reserved pieced diamonds and filler triangles as shown in the quilt assembly diagram. The piecing sequence is marked on the quilt assembly diagram. First add the filler triangles to the pieced diamonds and blocks as shown in stages 1–3, do this for all the triangles around the edges before starting the main sequence. Now start adding blocks together in the sequence

indicated, stages 4–35. Finally add the pieced borders as shown in stages 36–39 to complete the quilt.

FINISHING THE QUILT

Press the quilt top. Seam the backing pieces using a ¼in (6mm) seam allowance to form a piece approx. 73in x 79in (185.5cm x 200.5cm). Layer the quilt top, batting and backing and baste together (see page 139). Using toning machine quilting thread, quilt around each stage of the pieced diamonds and in the seams between each pieced diamond. Also quilt in the ditch of the border seams. Trim the quilt edges and attach the binding (see page 140).

Block Assembly Diagrams

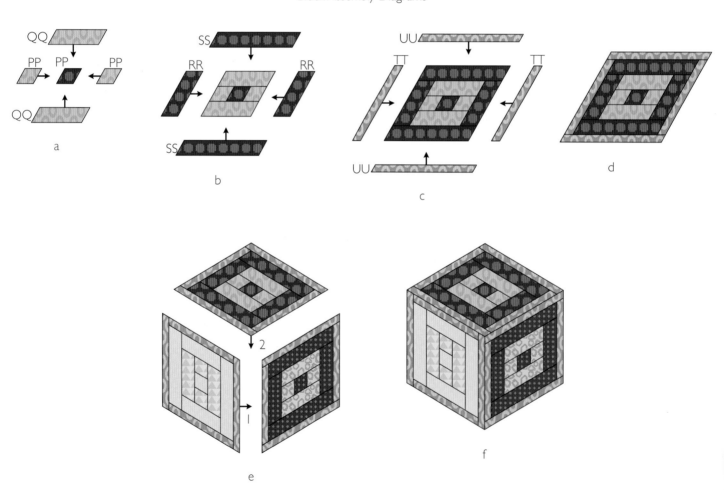

Quilt Assembly Diagram

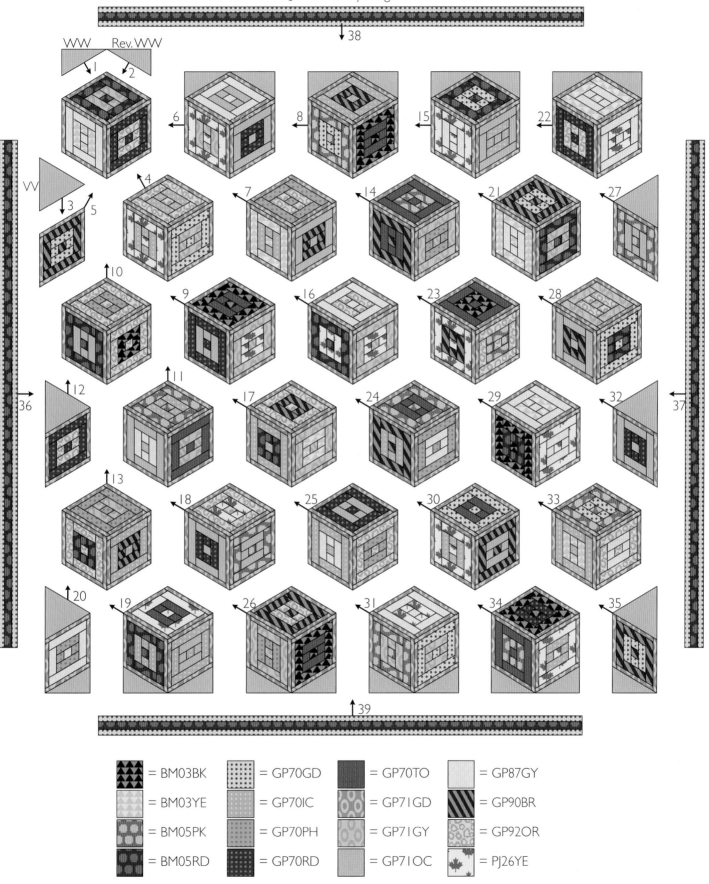

	= BM03BK		= GP70GD		= GP70TO		= GP87GY
	= BM03YE		= GP70IC		= GP71GD		= GP90BR
	= BM05PK		= GP70PH		= GP71GY		= GP92OR
	= BM05RD		= GP70RD		= GP71OC		= PJ26YE

Secret Forest Quilt ★

PAULINE SMITH

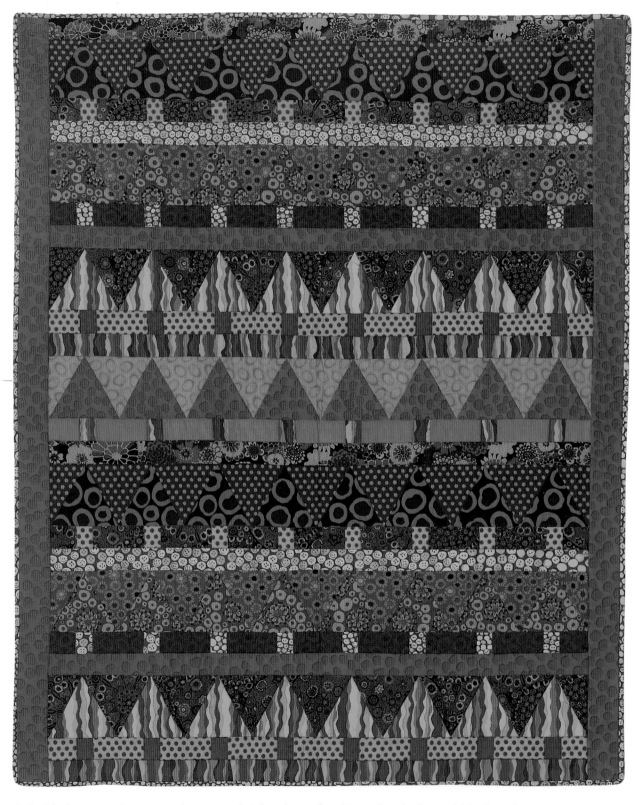

I decided on simple, strong shapes and rich colours for this quilt, which would look at home in a nursery.
I hope the rows of trees will appeal to a child's imagination and perhaps lead to a bedtime story.

SIZE OF QUILT
The finished quilt will measure approx.
56in × 68½in (142.25cm × 174cm).

MATERIALS
Patchwork Fabrics:
WAVES
Blue   BM04BL: ½yd (45cm)
Lipstick   BM04LP: ⅜yd (35cm)
DAPPLE
Blue   BM05BL: ⅞yd (80cm)
FISHLIPS
Purple   BM07PU: ½yd (45cm)
SPOT
Green   GP70GN: ⅜yd (35cm)
Magenta   GP70MG: ½yd (45cm)
Tobacco   GP70TO: ⅛yd (15cm)
ABORIGINAL DOTS
Ocean   GP71ON: ¼yd (25cm)
Periwinkle   GP71PE: ¼yd (25cm)
FLOWER DOT
Cobalt   GP87CB: ½yd (45cm)
ASIAN CIRCLES
Dark   GP89DK: ¼yd (25cm)
MILLEFIORE
Blue   GP92BL: ¾yd (70cm)
BUBBLE FLOWER
Magenta   GP97MG: ½yd (45cm)
BUTTONS
Green   GP101GN: ⅜yd (35cm)
SHOT COTTON
Viridian   SC55: ¼yd (25cm)

Backing Fabric: 3⅞yds (3.5m)
We suggest these fabrics for backing:
WAVES Lipstick, BM04LP
DAPPLE Blue, BM05BL

Binding:
BUTTONS
Green   GP101GN: ⅝yd (60cm)

Batting:
64in × 76in (162.5cm × 193cm).

Quilting Thread:
Toning machine quilting thread.

Templates:

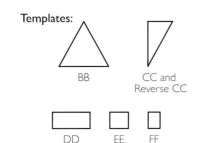

BB   CC and
            Reverse CC

DD   EE   FF

PATCH SHAPES
This quilt is pieced in rows. The 'tree' rows
are pieced using 2 triangle patch shapes
(Templates BB and CC and Reverse CC), the
main part of the row uses template BB
triangles and the ends of the rows are
completed with the template CC and
Reverse CC triangles. The 'trunk' rows are
pieced using 3 rectangle patch shapes
(Templates DD, EE, and FF), the main part of
the rows has template DD and FF rectangles
alternating and the row ends are completed
using template EE rectangles. The 'tree' and
'trunk' rows are interspaced with sashing
strips. Simple side borders complete the quilt.

CUTTING OUT
Cut the fabric in the order stated to prevent
waste. Reserve leftover strips and use for
later templates as appropriate.
Template CC and Reverse CC: Cut 6⅝in
(17cm) strips across the width of the fabric.
Cut 2 in GP70MG, GP87CB, GP92BL and 1
in GP71ON. Reverse the template by turning
it over and cut 2 in GP70MG, GP87CB,
GP92BL and 1 in GP71ON. Reserve the
remaining fabric strip and trim for Template
BB.
Template BB: Cut 6¼in (16cm) strips across
the width of the fabric. Each strip will give
you 9 patches per full width. Cut 16 in
BM04BL, BM07PU, GP97MG, 14 in GP70MG,
GP87CB, GP92BL, 8 in BM05BL and 7 in
GP91ON.
Sashing: Cut 2½in (6.25cm) strips across the
width of the fabric. Join as necessary and cut

2½in × 50½in (6.25cm × 128.25cm) sashing
strips. Cut 2 in BM04LP, BM05BL, GP89DK
and GP101GN.
Template DD: Cut 2½in (6.25cm) strips
across the width of the fabric. Each strip will
give you 7 patches per full width. Cut 14 in
GP70GN, GP71PE, GP92BL and 7 in SC55.
Template EE: Cut 2½in (6.25cm) strips
across the width of the fabric. Cut 4 in
GP70GN, GP71PE, GP92BL and 2 in SC55.
Template FF: Cut 2½in (6.25cm) strips across
the width of the fabric. Cut 16 in GP70GN,
GP70TO, GP101GN and 8 in BM04LP.

Borders: Cut 4 strips 3½in (9cm) wide
across the width of the fabric. Join as
necessary and cut 2 side borders 3½in ×
69in (9cm × 175.25cm) in BM05BL.

Binding: Cut 7 strips 2½in (6.5cm) wide
across the width of the fabric in GP101GN.

Backing: Cut 1 piece 40in × 64in (101.5cm ×
162.5cm) and 1 piece 37in × 64in (94cm ×
162.5cm).

MAKING THE QUILT
Use a ¼in (6mm) seam allowance
throughout. Refer to the quilt assembly
diagram for fabric placement. Lay out the
patches and separate into 14 pieced rows,
interspace as shown with the sashing strips
and join to form the quilt centre. Add the
side borders as shown in the quilt assembly
diagram to complete the quilt.

FINISHING THE QUILT
Press the quilt top. Seam the backing pieces
using a ¼in (6mm) seam allowance to form a
piece approx. 64in × 76in (162.5cm ×
193cm). Layer the quilt top, batting and
backing and baste together (see page 139).
Using toning machine quilting thread quilt in
the ditch throughout. Trim the quilt edges and
attach the binding (see page 140).

Quilt Assembly Diagram

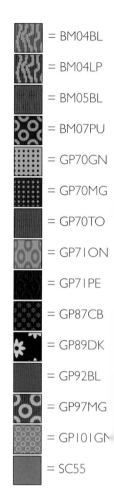

CC   BB   BB   Rev. CC

EE   FF   DD

= BM04BL

= BM04LP

= BM05BL

= BM07PU

= GP70GN

= GP70MG

= GP70TO

= GP71ON

= GP71PE

= GP87CB

= GP89DK

= GP92BL

= GP97MG

= GP101GN

= SC55

Tunisia Quilt ★★

KAFFE FASSETT

I spotted an embroidered appliqué textile in 'Hali', a magazine that specializes in carpets. The lozenge shaped pieces excited me. They were laid out in a diagonal pattern with flowers embroidered on each panel. I loved the way they slotted together. If I had time to do the quilt again I'd arrange contrasting colour panels in diagonal rows. This has a certain blowsy charm in warm pastels but I'd like to see it more like my inspiration, with more contrast in chalky and deeper colours.

SIZE OF QUILT
The finished quilt will measure approx.
91in x 95in (231cm x 241.5cm).

MATERIALS
Patchwork Fabrics:
Extra fabric has been allowed for fussy cutting this quilt.
ROMAN GLASS
Pink   GP01PK: ½yd (45cm)
ZINNIA
Pink   GP31PK: ⅝yd (60cm)
GUINEA FLOWER
Apricot   GP59AP: ½yd (45cm)
ASIAN CIRCLES
Green   GP89GN: ½yd (45cm)
Pink   GP89PK: ½yd (45cm)
CHEVRON STRIPE
Pink   GP90PK: ½yd (45cm)
BIG BLOOMS
Pink   GP91PK: ½yd (45cm)
RUSSIAN ROSE
Pastel   GP95PT: ⅝yd (60cm)
HENNA
Duck Egg   GP96DE: ⅝yd (60cm)
BUBBLE FLOWER
Summer   GP97SU: ½yd (45cm)
KIRMAN
Duck Egg   GP98DE: ⅝yd (60cm)
GARDEN PARTY
Celadon   PJ20CD: ⅝yd (60cm)
WALTZING MATILDA
Pastel   PJ22PT: ⅝yd (60cm)
TROPICAL
Celadon   PJ23CD: ½yd (45cm)
TULIP MANIA
Pastel   PJ24PT: ⅝yd (60cm)
LAYERED LEAVES
Celadon   PJ26CD: ⅝yd (60cm)
WOVEN MULTI STRIPE
Ivory   WMSIV: 2¾yds (2.5m)

Backing Fabric: 8yds (7.3m)
We suggest these fabrics for backing:
ASIAN CIRCLES Pink, GP89PK
TULIP MANIA Pastel, PJ24PT
TROPICAL Celadon, PJ23CD

Binding:
MIRAGE STRIPE
Yellow   GP104YE: ⅞yd (80cm)

Batting:
99in x 103in (251.5cm x 261.5cm).

Quilting Thread:
Hand quilting thread or perlé cotton embroidery thread in deep pink and grey.

Templates:

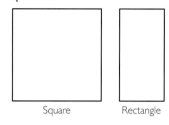

Square   Rectangle

Y   Z and Reverse Z   AA

PATCH SHAPES
The centre of this quilt is made up using 1 square patch shape (cut to size), 1 rectangle patch shape (cut to size), 1 triangle patch shape (Template AA) and 2 lozenge patch shapes (Templates Y and Z and Reverse Z). The lozenge shapes are pieced together with the triangles to form pieced rectangles which are interspaced with the squares and rectangles. The shapes are then joined into rows which in turn are joined to form the quilt. The careful fabric placement gives the illusion of Tunisian style tiles. The quilt is then surrounded with a simple border.

CUTTING OUT
Our usual 'strip cutting' method is not suitable for this quilt. We recommend drawing out the shapes onto the fabric before cutting to prevent waste.

Squares: Cut 12½in (31.75cm) squares, cut 3 in GP31PK, GP95PT, GP96DE, GP98DE, 2 in GP59AP, GP89GN, GP90PK, PJ20CD, PJ22PT, PJ23CD, PJ24PT, PJ26CD, 1 in GP01PK, GP89PK, GP91PK and GP97SU.

Rectangles: Cut 12½in x 6½in (31.75cm x 16.5cm) rectangles, cut 1 in GP01PK, GP91PK, PJ20CD, PJ22PT, PJ24PT and PJ26CD.

Template Y: Cut 5 in GP95PT, GP96DE, 4 in GP01PK, GP31PK, GP89PK, GP91PK, GP97SU, GP98DE, PJ20CD, PJ22PT, PJ24PT, PJ26CD, 3 in GP59AP, GP89GN, GP90PK and PJ23CD.

Template Z and Reverse Z: Cut 1 in GP01PK, GP89PK, GP91PK, GP97SU, PJ20CD, PJ22PT, PJ24PT, and PJ26CD. Reverse the template by turning it over, cut 1 in GP01PK, GP89PK, GP91PK, GP97SU, PJ20CD, PJ22PT,

PJ24PT, and PJ26CD.

Template AA: Cut the triangles with the straight grain of the fabric along the long side of the triangle. Cut 6 in GP31PK, GP95PT, GP96DE, GP98DE, 5 in PJ20CD, PJ22PT, PJ24PT, PJ26CD, 4 in GP59AP, GP89GN, GP90PK, PJ23CD, 3 in GP01PK, GP91PK, 2 in GP89PK and GP97SU.

Borders: Cut 6in (15.25cm) strips down the length of the fabric carefully, keeping the stripes straight. Cut 2 strips 6in x 91½in (232.5cm) for the quilt top and bottom and 2 strips 6in x 84½in (214.5cm) for the quilt sides in WMSIV.

Binding: Cut 10 strips 2½in (6.5cm) wide across the width of the fabric in GP104YE.

Backing: Cut 2 pieces 40in x 99in (101.5cm x 251.5cm) 2 pieces 40in x 24in (101.5cm x 61cm) and 1 piece 24in x 20in (61cm x 51cm) in backing fabric.

MAKING THE BLOCKS
Use a ¼in (6mm) seam allowance throughout. Referring to the quilt assembly diagram for fabric placement piece a total of 31 blocks using the template Y and template AA patches as shown in block assembly diagram a and b. The finished block can be seen in diagram c. Next piece 8 half blocks using the template Z and reverse Z and remaining template AA patches as shown in diagram d, the finished half block can be seen in diagram e.

MAKING THE QUILT
Refer to the quilt assembly diagram for fabric placement. Lay out the pieced blocks with the squares and rectangles as shown in the quilt assembly diagram. Separate into 7 rows and join the rows to form the quilt centre. Add the side borders then the top and bottom borders to complete the quilt.

FINISHING THE QUILT
Press the quilt top. Seam the backing pieces using a ¼in (6mm) seam allowance to form a piece approx. 99in x 103in (251.5cm x 261.5cm). Layer the quilt top, batting and backing and baste together (see page 139). Using deep pink hand quilting thread or perlé embroidery thread quilt the quilt centre as shown in the quilting diagram. Quilt the borders as shown using grey thread. Trim the quilt edges and attach the binding (see page 140).

Block Assembly Diagrams

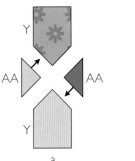 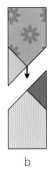 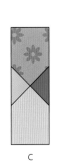

Reverse Z

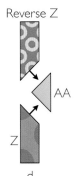 

a   b   c   d   e

Quilting Diagram

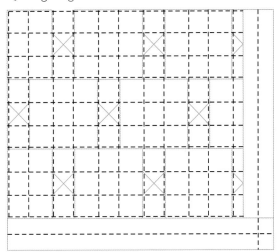

Quilt Assembly Diagram

Square

Rectangle   Square

= GP01PK	= GP91PK	= PJ22PT
= GP31PK	= GP95PT	= PJ23CD
= GP59AP	= GP96DE	= PJ24PT
= GP89GN	= GP97SU	= PJ26CD
= GP89PK	=GP98DE	= WMSIV
= GP90PK	= PJ20CD	

Gameboard Quilt ★★

LIZA PRIOR LUCY

Liza has used highly contrasting fabrics and a kaleidoscopic layout to create a quilt with real drama.

SIZE OF QUILT
The finished quilt will measure approx.
90in × 90in (228.5cm × 228.5cm).

MATERIALS
Patchwork Fabrics:
ROMAN GLASS
Blue/White   GP01BW: ³⁄₈yd (35cm)
PAPERWEIGHT
Cobalt   GP20CB: ½yd (45cm)
LOTUS LEAF
Blue   GP29BL: 2yds (1.8m)
PAISLEY JUNGLE
Blue   GP60BL: ¾yd (70cm)
SPOT
Sky   GP70SK: 4⅛yds (3.8m)
MILLEFIORE
Blue   GP92BL: 1¼yds (1.15m)

Backing Fabric: 7yds (6.4m)
We suggest these fabrics for backing:
ROMAN GLASS Blue, GP01BW
SPOT Sky, GP70SK
MILLEFIORE Blue, GP92BL

Binding:
ABORIGINAL DOTS
Periwinkle   GP71PE: ⅞yd (80cm)

Batting:
98in × 98in (249cm × 249cm).

Quilting Thread:
White and navy blue machine quilting threads.

Templates:

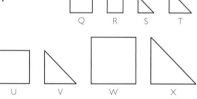

PATCH SHAPES
The centre of this quilt is a pieced checkerboard panel which uses a square patch shape (Template Q). The centre is then surrounded with a series of pieced triangle sections. The first 'round' of triangles are pieced using a square patch shape (Template R) and a triangle patch shape (Template S). The second 'round' of triangles are pieced reusing the square patch shape from the centre checkerboard (Template Q) and a triangle patch shape (Template T). The third and fourth 'rounds' each uses a square patch shape (Templates U and W) and a triangle patch shape (Templates V and X).

CUTTING OUT
Cut the fabric in the order stated, we have listed the cutting for the 'rounds' of pieced triangles and the checkerboard centre separately working from the largest to the smallest patches to prevent waste.

Pieced Triangles 'Round' 4
Template X: Cut 8⅜in (21.25cm) strips across the width of the fabric. Each strip will give you 8 patches per full width. Cut 24 in GP29BL.
Template W: Cut 8in (20.25cm) strips across the width of the fabric. Each strip will give you 5 patches per full width. Cut 36 in GP70SK and 24 in GP29BL.

Pieced Triangles 'Round' 3
Template V: Cut 6¼in (16cm) strips across the width of the fabric. Each strip will give you 12 patches per full width. Cut 24 in GP92BL.
Template U: Cut 5⅞in (15cm) strips across the width of the fabric. Each strip will give you 6 patches per full width. Cut 36 in GP70SK and 24 in GP92BL.

Pieced Triangles 'Round' 2
Template T: Cut 4⅝in (11.75cm) strips across the width of the fabric. Each strip will give you 16 patches per full width. Cut 24 in GP60BL.
Template Q: Cut 4¼in (10.75cm) strips across the width of the fabric. Each strip will give you 9 patches per full width. Cut 36 in GP70SK and 24 in GP60BL.

Checkerboard Centre
Template Q: Cut 4¼in (10.75cm) strips across the width of the fabric. Each strip will give you 9 patches per full width. Cut 18 in GP01BW and GP70SK.

Pieced Triangles 'Round' 1
Template S: Cut 3½in (9cm) strips across the width of the fabric. Each strip will give you 22 patches per full width. Cut 24 in GP20CB.
Template R: Cut 3⅛in (8cm) strips across the width of the fabric. Each strip will give you 12 patches per full width. Cut 36 in GP70SK and 24 in GP20CB.

Binding: Cut 9 strips 2½in (6.5cm) wide across the width of the fabric in GP71PE.

Backing: Cut 2 pieces 40in × 98in (101.5cm × 249cm) and 1 piece 98in ×19in (249cm × 48.25cm) in backing fabric.

MAKING THE QUILT
Use a ¼in (6mm) seam allowance throughout. Starting with the centre checkerboard panel, piece it in rows as shown in block assembly diagram a. Next piece 4 triangle sections for round 1 as shown in block assembly diagram b. The finished section can be seen in diagram c. Add the pieced triangle sections to the

Block Assembly Diagrams

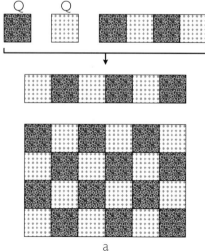

a

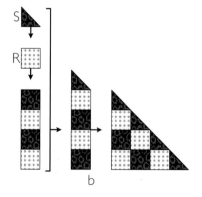

b

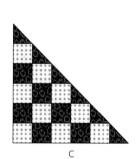

c

checkerboard centre panel as indicated in the quilt assembly diagram, working on 2 opposite sides and then the other 2 sides. Rounds 2, 3 and 4 are pieced and added to the quilt centre in the same way.

FINISHING THE QUILT
Press the quilt top. Seam the backing pieces using a ¼in (6mm) seam allowance to form a piece approx. 98in × 98in (249cm × 249cm). Layer the quilt top, batting and backing and baste together (see page 139). Using white machine quilting thread in the light areas and navy blue thread in the dark areas free motion meander quilt as you prefer. Trim the quilt edges and attach the binding (see page 140).

Quilt Assembly Diagram

= GP01BW	= GP29BL	= GP70SK
= GP20CB	= GP60BL	= GP92BL

Enclosed 4 Patch Quilt ★

Roberta Horton

Lovely botanicals fenced in by 9 patches... simple, elegant, strong. The beautiful fabric does all the work, what more could you want?

SIZE OF QUILT
The finished quilt will measure approx.
75in × 88¾in (190.5cm × 225.5cm).

MATERIALS
Patchwork Fabrics:
ABORIGINAL DOTS
Plum   GP71PL: 2½yds (2.3m)
GLORY ROSE
Red   PJ21RD: 1¼yds (1.15m)
WALTZING MATILDA
Emerald   PJ22ED: 1¼yds (1.15m)
TROPICAL
Emerald   PJ23ED: 1½yds (1.4m)
TULIP MANIA
Green   PJ24GN: 1¾yds (1.6m)

Backing Fabric: 6yds (5.5m)
We suggest these fabrics for backing:
TULIP MANIA Red, PJ24RD
LAYERED LEAVES Rust, PJ26RU

Binding:
WAVES
Circus   BM03CR: ¾yd (70cm)

Batting:
83in × 95in (211cm × 241.5cm).

Quilting Thread:
Purple and red machine quilting threads.

Templates:

F   G   H

PATCH SHAPES
The centre of this quilt is made of 4 patch blocks using 1 square patch shape (Template F). The 4 patch blocks are straight set, surrounded and interspaced with sashing units which are pieced using 1 rectangle patch shape (Template H), the sashing corner posts are 9 patch blocks, pieced using 1 square patch shape (Template G). The quilt is finished with a border with pieced corner posts, again using 1 square patch shape (Template G).

CUTTING OUT
Template F: Cut 4½in (11.5cm) strips across the width of the fabric. Each strip will give you 8 patches per full width. Cut 60 in PJ21RD and PJ22ED.
Template G: Cut 1¾in (4.5cm) strips across the width of the fabric. Each strip will give you 22 patches per full width. Cut 258 in PJ24GN and 220 in GP71PL.
Template H: Cut 1¾in (4.5cm) strips across the width of the fabric. Each strip will give you 4 patches per full width. Cut 142 in GP71PL and 71 in PJ24GN.

Borders: Cut 7 strips 6¾in (17.25cm) wide across the width of the fabric in PJ23ED. Join the strips as necessary and cut 2 strips 6¾in × 74¾in (17.25cm × 190cm) for the quilt sides and 2 strips 6¾in × 63in (17.25cm × 160cm) for the quilt top and bottom.

Binding: Cut 9 strips 2½in (6.5cm) wide across the width of the fabric in BM03CR.

Backing: Cut 2 pieces 40in × 95in (101.5cm × 241.5cm), 2 pieces 40in × 4in (101.5cm × 10.25cm) and 1 piece 4in × 16in (10.25cm × 40.5cm) in backing fabric.

MAKING THE BLOCKS AND SASHING
Use a ¼in (6mm) seam allowance throughout. Refer to the quilt assembly diagram for fabric placement. Piece a total of 30 4 patch blocks as shown in block assembly diagram a, the finished block can be seen in diagram b. For the sashing corner posts piece a total of 42 9 patch blocks as shown in diagram c, the finished block is shown in diagram d. Piece a total of 71 sashing units as shown in diagram e, the finished unit can be seen in diagram f. Finally make up the 4 border corner posts as shown in block assembly diagram g, the finished block can be seen in diagram h.

MAKING THE QUILT
Arrange the 4 patch blocks, sashing units and 9 patch corner posts as shown in the quilt assembly diagram. Separate and join into rows as shown. Join the rows to complete the quilt centre.

Add the side borders to the quilt centre. Join a border corner post to each end of the top and bottom borders then add to the quilt centre to complete the quilt as shown in the quilt assembly diagram.

FINISHING THE QUILT
Press the quilt top. Seam the backing pieces using a ¼in (6mm) seam allowance to form a

Block Assembly Diagrams

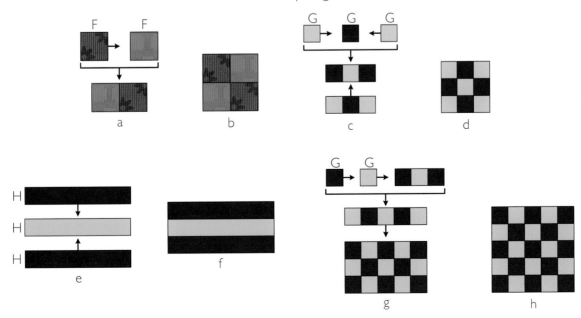

a   b   c   d

e   f   g   h

piece approx. 83in × 95in (211cm × 241.5cm).Layer the quilt top, batting and backing and baste together (see page 139). Using purple machine quilting thread, quilt in the ditch in all the sashing, 9 patch and border corner post block seams. Using red thread quilt in the ditch in the 4 patch blocks, also add an 'X' in each quarter of the 4 patch. Quilt the borders with 4 parallel serpentine stitching lines using red thread. Trim the quilt edges and attach the binding (see page 140).

Quilt Assembly Diagram

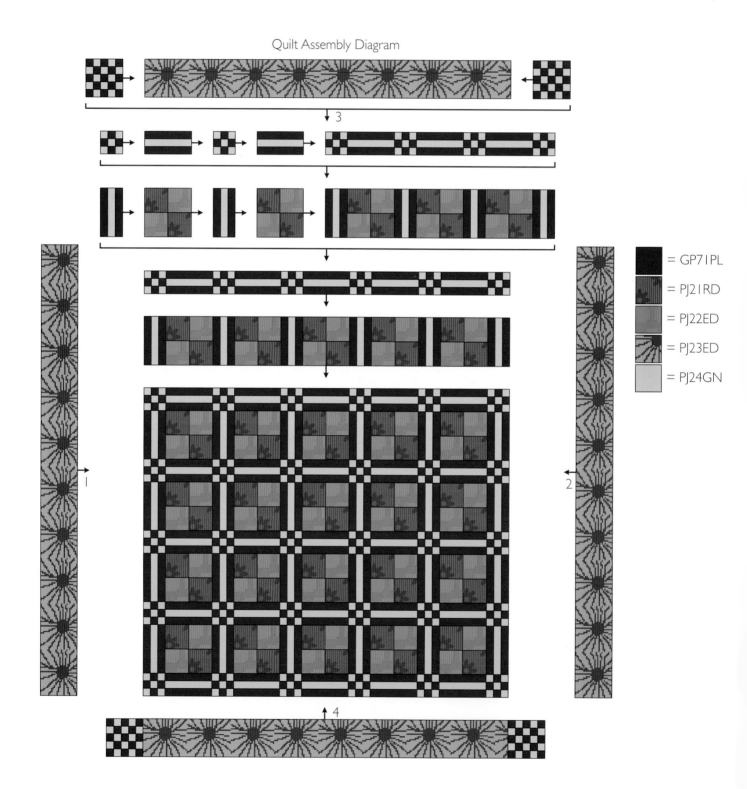

= GP71PL

= PJ21RD

= PJ22ED

= PJ23ED

= PJ24GN

Porch Weave Quilt ★★

KAFFE FASSETT

On my annual Christmas trip to my family in California I took a walk through San Francisco. At the entrance to a Victorian building I saw a great layout of tiles that so captivated me I did a quick sketch on the back of an envelope. Working it out in fabric was a little tricky but I think you will all agree it is a very clever use of Bricks and Squares that could be done in endless combos of colour.

SIZE OF QUILT
The finished quilt will measure approx.
76½in x 103½in (194.5cm x 263cm).

MATERIALS
Patchwork Fabrics:
FISH LIPS
Purple BM07PU: ¼yd (25cm)
ZINNIA
Blue GP31BL: ⅜yd (35cm)
ASIAN CIRCLES
Dark GP89DK: ⅜yd (35cm)
BUBBLE FLOWER
Teal GP97TE: ¼yd (25cm)
SUZANI
Brown GP105BR: ¼yd (25cm)
Pink GP105PK: ⅜yd (35cm)
Purple GP105PU: ¼yd (25cm)
SPRAYS
Black GP107BK: ¼yd (25cm)
Brown GP107BR: ¼yd (25cm)
GLORY ROSE
Maroon PJ21MR: ⅜yd (35cm)
WOVEN MULTI STRIPE
Fuchsia WMSFU: 3⅛yds (2.9m)
Teal WMSTE: 3⅛yds (2.9m)

Backing Fabric: 7½yds (6.9m)
We suggest these fabrics for backing:
GLORY ROSE Maroon, PJ21MR
SUZANI Pink, GP105PK
ASIAN CIRCLES Dark, GP89DK

Binding:
WOVEN BROAD STRIPE
Fuchsia WBSFU: ⅞yd (80cm)

Batting:
84in x 111in (213.5cm x 282cm).

Quilting Thread:
Toning machine quilting thread.

PATCH SHAPES
This quilt is pieced using 1 square patch shape and 2 rectangle patch shapes, all are cut to size and no templates are provided for these very simple shapes. Careful cutting and matching of the striped fabrics creates the illusion of a woven lattice when in fact the quilt is pieced in simple rows. We recommend using a design wall for laying out this quilt.

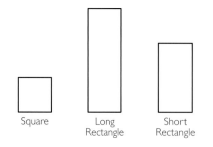

Square   Long Rectangle   Short Rectangle

CUTTING OUT
WOVEN STRIPE FABRICS ONLY:
The stripe design runs down the length of the fabric, cut a single layer of fabric at a time to keep the stripes running true along the rectangle shapes. Please read the whole cutting instruction carefully before you start.
Long Rectangles: Cut 3 strips 14in (35.5cm) x the width of the fabric in WMSFU and WMSTE. Cutting with the stripes along the length of each rectangle cut a total of 21 rectangles 5in x 14in (12.75cm x 35.5cm) in WMSFU and WMSTE. Reserve leftover strips for cutting Squares.
Short Rectangles: Cut 1 strip 9½in (24.25cm) x the width of the fabric in WMSFU and WMSTE. Cutting with the stripes along the length of each rectangle cut a total of 6 rectangles 5in x 9½in (12.75cm x 24.25cm) in WMSFU and WMSTE.
Squares: Cut a piece of fabric 47in (119.5cm) x the width of the fabric in WMSFU and WMSTE. Cut 8 strips 5in (12.75cm) wide down the length of the fabric. From each strip cut 9 squares 5in x 5in (12.75cm x 12.75cm). As you cut the squares pin in sets of 3 so that they will match when stitched in the quilt (see Making The Quilt for more details). This will give you 72 squares in each

colourway. From the leftover strips from cutting the Long Rectangles, cut 5 squares in WMSTE and 4 squares in WMSFU. Total 77 squares in WMSTE and 76 in WMSFU.
ALL OTHER FABRICS:
Squares: Cut 5in (12.75cm) strips across the width of the fabric. Each strip will give you 8 patches per full width. From these cut 5in (12.75cm) squares. Cut 12 in GP31BL, GP105PK, PJ21MR, 9 in GP89DK, 8 in BM07PU, GP105PU, 7 in GP105BR, GP107BK, GP107BR and 6 in GP97TE.

Binding: Cut 10 strips 2½in (6.5cm) wide across the width of the fabric in WBSFU.

Backing: Cut 2 pieces 40in x 84in (101.5cm x 213.5cm) and 1 piece 32in x 84in (81.25cm x 213.5cm) in backing fabric.

MAKING THE QUILT
Use a ¼in (6mm) seam allowance throughout. Refer to the quilt assembly diagram for fabric placement. Arrange all the patches as shown in the quilt assembly diagram, we recommend using a design wall for this. Where 3 squares (or 2 squares on the top or bottom edge of the quilt) of WMSFU or WMSTE are used in a vertical row to give the illusion of a Long Rectangle use sets of 3 cut from the same strip for the best match. Separate the patches into 11 rows and join. Join the rows to complete the quilt.

FINISHING THE QUILT
Press the quilt top. Seam the backing pieces using a ¼in (6mm) seam allowance to form a piece approx. 84in x 111in (213.5cm x 282cm). Layer the quilt top, batting and backing and baste together (see page 139). Using toning thread machine quilt in the ditch around the printed fabric squares. Then quilt serpentine curvy lines horizontally and vertically in the Woven Multi Stripe lattice. Trim the quilt edges and attach the binding (see page 140).

Quilt Assembly Diagram

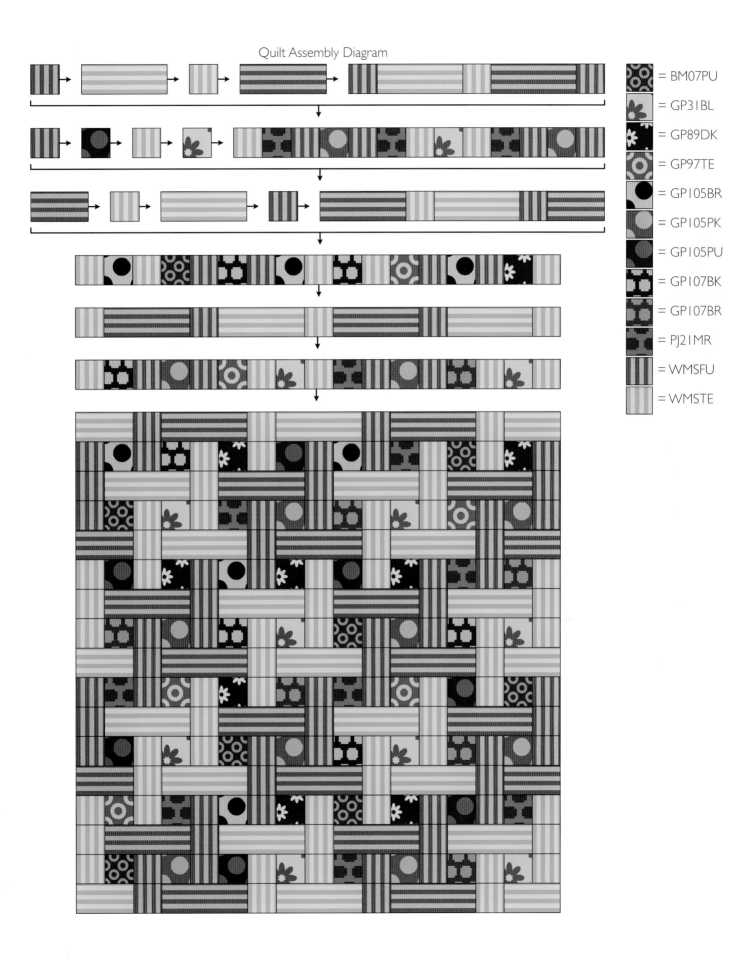

= BM07PU

= GP31BL

= GP89DK

= GP97TE

= GP105BR

= GP105PK

= GP105PU

= GP107BK

= GP107BR

= PJ21MR

= WMSFU

= WMSTE

Persian Garden Quilt ★

KAFFE FASSETT

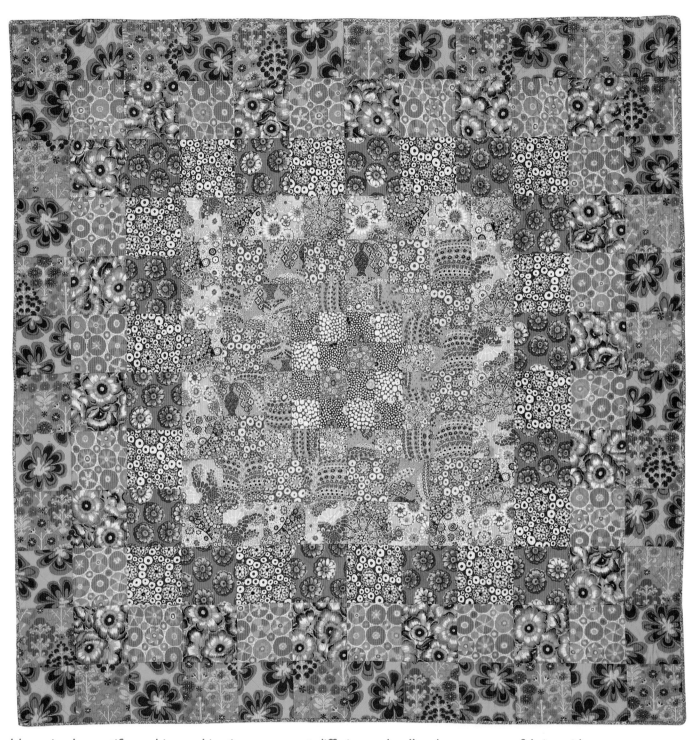

I love circular motifs used in combination, so you get differing scales. I've done so many fabrics with circular themes that putting them all together was a natural step for me. I chose pastel fabrics for this version, but I now feel it could be much stronger if done in a dark smouldering palette. I hope you can have a go now we have so many circular fabrics in the collection in deeper tones.

SIZE OF QUILT
The finished quilt will measure approx.
96in × 96in (244cm × 244cm).

MATERIALS
Patchwork Fabrics:
FLORA
Blue   BM11BL: 1⅝yds (1.5m)
ROMAN GLASS
Pink   GP01PK: ¼yd (25cm)
PAPERWEIGHT
Pastel   GP20PT: ⅜yd (35cm)
ZINNIA
Pink   GP31PK: 1⅛yds (1m)
GUINEA FLOWER
Blue   GP59BL: ¼yd (25cm)
ASIAN CIRCLES
Pink   GP89PK: ⅝yd (60cm)
MILLEFIORE
Pastel   GP92PT: ⅝yd (60cm)
BUBBLE FLOWER
Blue   GP97BL: 1⅛yds (1m)
Summer   GP97SU: ½yd (45cm)
PERSIAN VASE
Duck Egg   GP100DE: ⅜yd (35cm)
Grey   GP100GY: ½yd (45cm)
BUTTONS
Blue   GP101BL: ¼yd (25cm)
SUZANI
Pink   GP105PK: 1⅜yds (1.3m)
SPRAYS
Taupe   GP107TA: 1⅝yds (1.5m)
WALTZING MATILDA
Pastel   PJ22PT: 1⅜yds (1.3m)

Backing Fabric: 8⅜yds (7.7m)
We suggest these fabrics for backing:
PAPERWEIGHT Pastel, GP20PT
SUZANI Pink, GP105PK
SPRAYS Taupe, GP107TA

Binding:
ROMAN GLASS
Pink   GP01PK: ⅞yd (80cm)

Batting:
104in × 104in (264cm × 264cm).

Quilting Thread:
Coats Star Machine Quilting Thread, shade: Sherbet 882, this is a variegated thread with pastel pinks and mauves.
Alternatively use toning machine quilting thread.

PATCH SHAPES
This quilt is pieced using 3 sizes of square patches, all are cut to size and no templates are provided for these very simple shapes. The centre section of the quilt uses a small square and is pieced in rows. The middle section of the quilt uses a medium square and is pieced into sections and then added to the centre. The outer section of the quilt uses a large square and is again pieced into sections and added to the centre. This is an ideal quilt for a beginner.

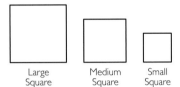
Large Square   Medium Square   Small Square

CUTTING OUT
Small Squares: Cut 4½in (11.5cm) strips across the width of the fabric. Each strip will give you 8 patches per full width. From these cut 4½in (11.5cm) squares. Cut 10 in GP20PT, GP100DE, 8 in GP59BL, 6 in GP101BL and 2 in GP01PK.
Medium Squares: Cut 6½in (16.5cm) strips across the width of the fabric. Each strip will give you 6 patches per full width. From these cut 6½in (16.5cm) squares. Cut 14 in GP89PK, GP92PT, 10 in GP97SU and GP100GY.
Large Squares: Cut 8½in (21.5cm) strips across the width of the fabric. Each strip will

give you 4 patches per full width. From these cut 8½in (21.5cm) squares. Cut 22 in BM11BL, GP107TA, 18 in GP105PK, PJ22PT, 14 in GP31PK and GP97BL.

Binding: Cut 10 strips 2½in (6.5cm) wide across the width of the fabric in GP01PK.

Backing: Cut 2 pieces 40in × 104in (101.5cm × 264cm), 2 pieces 40in × 25in (101.5cm × 63.5cm) and 1 piece 25in × 25in (63.5cm × 63.5cm) in backing fabric. Note: For a quirky look to the backing you could cut the 25in (63.5cm) square from a different fabric and piece the backing with the contrasting square in the centre.

MAKING THE QUILT
Use a ¼in (6mm) seam allowance throughout. Refer to the quilt assembly diagram for fabric placement. Working first on the centre section, arrange the small squares into 6 rows of 6 small squares. Join the squares to form the rows and then join the rows to form the centre section. Next arrange the medium squares as shown in the quilt assembly diagram. Join the squares into pairs, and then into sections. Join the sections to the quilt centre as shown. Finally arrange the large squares as shown in the quilt assembly diagram. Join the squares, this time in 3's and then into sections. Join them to the quilt sections as shown to complete the quilt.

FINISHING THE QUILT
Press the quilt top. Seam the backing pieces using a ¼in (6mm) seam allowance to form a piece approx. 104in × 104in (264cm × 264cm). Layer the quilt top, batting and backing and baste together (see page 139). Using variegated (as stated above) or toning thread machine quilt in the ditch throughout, also quilt in a crosshatch pattern across the medium and large squares. Trim the quilt edges and attach the binding (see page 140).

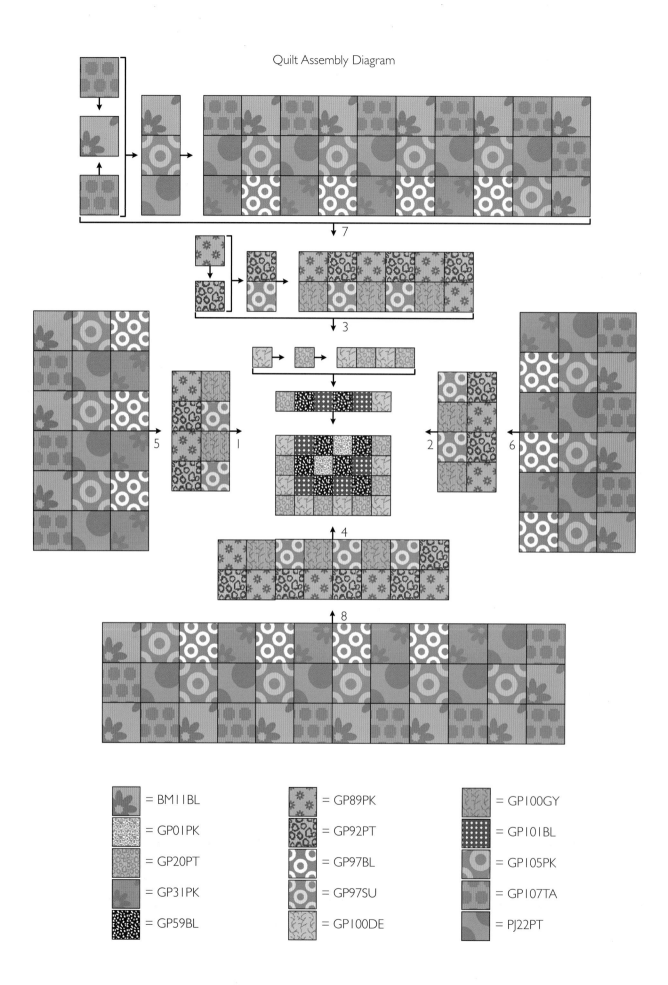

= BM11BL

= GP01PK

= GP20PT

= GP31PK

= GP59BL

= GP89PK

= GP92PT

= GP97BL

= GP97SU

= GP100DE

= GP100GY

= GP101BL

= GP105PK

= GP107TA

= PJ22PT

Beyond the Border Quilt ★ ★

BRANDON MABLY

The Gee's Bend quilters are a breath of fresh air when it comes to placing colour, form and pattern. I tried doing a line drawing to try and understand how they decided upon their placement. It became evident they don't plan in this. Because this quilt is machine sewn we have ended up with straight lines, but I'm really pleased with how my fabrics work with one another in a fresh and unexpected way. Also I think the title is apt as it says what the Gee's Bend quilters are – beyond the borders.

SIZE OF QUILT
The finished quilt will measure approx.
76in x 84in (193cm x 213.5cm).

MATERIALS
Patchwork Fabrics:

STRAWS
Grey	BM08GY: ¼yd (25cm)
Lime	BM08LM: ¼yd (25cm)

SPLASH
Pastel	BM09PT: ½yd (45cm)

BONES
Yellow	BM10YE: 1¼yds (1.15m)

FLORA
Blue	BM11BL: ⅝yd (60cm)
Pink	BM11PK: 2⅛yds (1.9m)

SCALES
Brown	BM12BR: 1yd (90cm)
Lime	BM12LM: 2¼yds (2m)

WOODEAR
Ochre	GP99OC: ⅝yd (60cm)

Backing Fabric: 5⅞yds (5.4m)
We suggest these fabrics for backing:
FLORA Pink, BM11PK
SCALES Lime, BM12LM

Binding:
STRAWS
Grey	BM08GY: ¾yd (70cm)

Batting:
84in x 92in (213.5cm x 233.5cm).

Quilting Threads:
Toning machine quilting thread.
Toning hand quilting thread or perlé cotton embroidery thread.

PATCH SHAPES
This quilt is assembled from the centre out using a selection of strips (cut to size). To get the look of Brandon's quilt some of the fabrics are cut down the length of the fabric and others across the width, with a bit of pattern matching and joining, so please read the cutting instructions carefully before you start.

CUTTING OUT
Please read all the cutting instructions carefully before you start.
Cut strips across the width of the fabric unless otherwise stated and cut the pieces in the order stated to avoid waste.

Piece A: Cut a rectangle 8½in x 32½in (21.5cm x 82.5cm) in BM11BL.
Piece B: Cut 2 rectangles 6½in x 32½in (16.5cm x 82.5cm) in BM09PT.
Piece C: Down the length of the fabric cut 2 rectangles 6½in x 20½in (16.5cm x 52cm) in BM12BR.
Piece D: Down the length of the fabric cut a rectangle 6½in x 26½in (16.5cm x 67.25cm) in BM12BR.
Piece E: Cut a rectangle 6½in x 8½in (16.5cm x 21.5cm) BM08GY.
Piece F: Cut a rectangle 6½in x 10½in (16.5cm x 26.75cm) BM08LM.
Piece G: Down the length of the fabric cut a rectangle 6½in x 32½in (16.5cm x 82.5cm) in BM12BR.
Piece H: Cut a square 6½in x 6½in (16.5cm x 16.5cm) in BM08LM.
Piece I: Cut a square 6½in x 6½in (16.5cm x 16.5cm) in BM08GY.
Piece J: Down the length of the fabric cut a rectangle 6½in x 32½in (16.5cm x 82.5cm) in BM10YE.
Piece L: Down the length of the fabric cut a rectangle 6½in x 40½in (16.5cm x 103cm) in BM10YE.
Piece K: From the remaining BM10YE fabric fussy cut strips across the width and join with the circles in the fabric design centred (see the photograph for detail) cut a rectangle 8½in x 50½in (21.5cm x 128.25cm) in BM10YE.
Piece M: Cut 2 strips 8½in wide across the width of the fabric in GP99OC. Join the strips and cut a rectangle 8½in x 56½in (21.5cm x 143.5cm).

Piece N: Cut a rectangle 6½in x 40½in (16.5cm x 103cm) in BM12LM.
Piece O: Cut a rectangle 6½in x 8½in (16.5cm x 21.5cm) BM12BR.
Piece P: From the remaining BM12LM fabric, down the length of the fabric cut 2 rectangles 6½in x 68½in (16.5cm x 174cm) in BM12LM.
Piece Q: From the remaining BM12LM fabric, down the length of the fabric cut 1 rectangle 6½in x 48½in (16.5cm x 123.25cm) in BM12LM.
Pieces R and S: Down the length of the fabric cut 2 rectangles 8½in x 68½in (21.5 x 174cm) and 2 rectangles 8½in x 60½in (21.5 x 153.75cm) in BM11PK.
Piece T: Cut 4 squares 8½in x 8½in (21.5cm x 21.5cm) in BM11BL.

Binding: Cut 9 strips 2½in (6.5cm) wide across the width of the fabric in BM08GY.

Backing: Cut 2 pieces 40in x 84in (101.5cm x 213.5cm), 2 pieces 40in x 13in (101.5cm x 33cm) and 1 piece 13in x 5in (33cm x 12.75cm) in backing fabric.

MAKING THE QUILT
Use a ¼in (6mm) seam allowance throughout. Assemble the quilt in the order indicated in the quilt assembly diagram.

FINISHING THE QUILT
Press the quilt top. Seam the backing pieces using a ¼in (6mm) seam allowance to form a piece approx. 84in x 92in (213.5cm x 233.5cm). Layer the quilt top, batting and backing and baste together (see page 139). Using toning machine quilting thread, stitch in the ditch along all seam lines. Using toning hand quilting quilting thread or perlé cotton embroidery thread hand quilt approximately 1½in (3.75cm) in from the seams on the narrow rectangles and 2½in (6.25cm) from the seams and border edges on the wide rectangles. Trim the quilt edges and attach the binding (see page 140).

Quilt Assembly Diagram

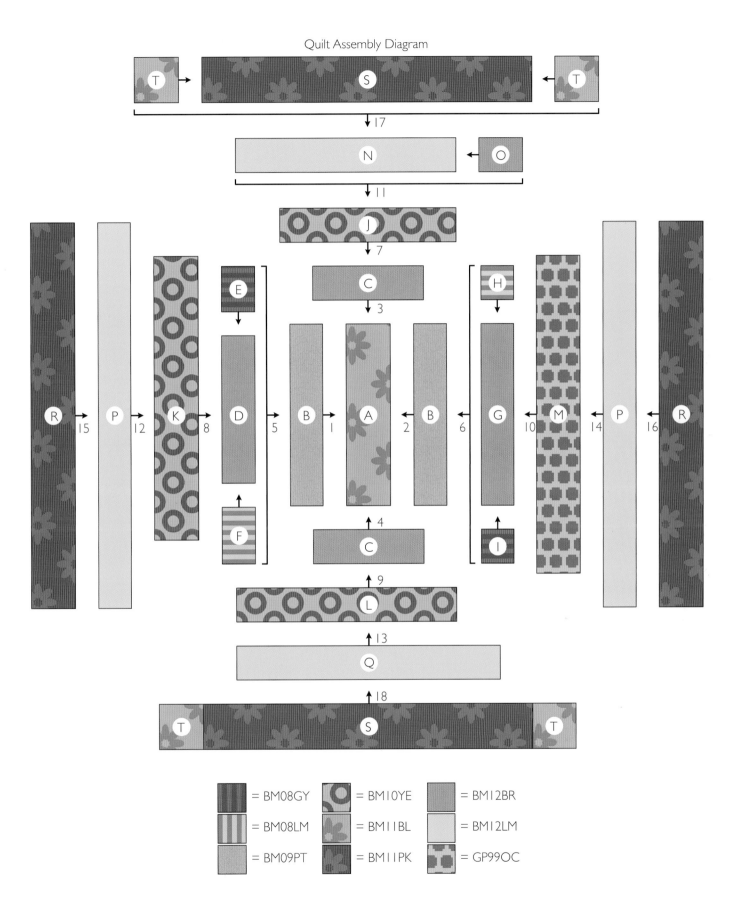

= BM08GY   = BM10YE   = BM12BR

= BM08LM   = BM11BL   = BM12LM

= BM09PT   = BM11PK   = GP99OC

X Factor Quilt ★★

KAFFE FASSETT

This is my favourite layout in this book and hence its place on our cover. When I spotted a vintage silk quilt on E Bay I had to have it. It felt as fresh and modern as a Picasso painting, yet done in the 1800's. The simple layout of the diagonal stripe excites me most and how it comes together to create all these various moods. I'm knitting a version as a bed cover and it's just as exciting as creating the quilt.

SIZE OF QUILT
The finished quilt will measure approx.
79½in x 90½in (202cm x 230cm).

MATERIALS
Patchwork Fabrics:
TENTS
Black   BM03BK: ½yd (45cm)
SPOT
Green   GP70GN: ¼yd (25cm)
Duck Egg   GP70DE: ¾yd (70cm)
ABORIGINAL DOTS
Grey   GP71GY: ⅜yd (35cm)
Plum   GP71PL: 1yd (90cm)
Periwinkle   GP71PE: ⅜yd (35cm)
FLOWER DOT
Grey   GP87GY: ⅞yd (80cm)
MILLEFIORE
Blue   GP92BL: ⅜yd (35cm)
SHOT COTTON
Raspberry   SC08: 2½yds (2.3m)
Sunshine   SC35: ¾yd (70cm)
Scarlet   SC44: ¼yd (25cm)
Aegean   SC46: ⅝yd 60cm)
Nut   SC53: ¼yd (25cm)
Sky   SC62: 1yd (90cm)
Coal   SC63: 2¾yds (2.5m)
Butter   SC64: 1½yds (1.4m)
Pudding   SC68: ⅞yd (80cm)
Mulberry   SC73: ⅝yd (60cm)
Vermillion   SC74: ½yd (45cm)

Backing Fabric: 6⅝yds (6.1m)
WOVEN BOLD STRIPE Fuchsia, WBSFU

Binding:
MOVEN MULTI STRIPE
Fuchsia   WMSFU: ¾yd (70cm)

Batting:
87in x 98in (221cm x 249cm).

Quilting Thread:
Toning hand quilting thread.

Templates:

XX

PATCH SHAPES
Strip sets of 9 fabrics are joined and then cut using a square shape (Template XX). Four of these squares are joined to form blocks. The centre fabric in the strip set (usually a blue, pink or yellow strip) then comes together to form a graphic 'X' shape in each block. We have coloured the diagram very simply for this quilt showing only the graphic 'X' shapes

as this is the most important feature. There are a few 'rogue' blocks where the 'X' shapes are mixed and a few of the fabrics were pieced wrong side up to add interest. Spare blocks are made using the leftovers from cutting with the addition of an extra strip of fabric. Some of these are pieced into 'rogue' blocks and some are used to make inner borders for the right side and bottom of the quilt centre. The quilt centre is then surrounded with a pieced border made from leftover fabrics. We recommend using transparent plastic for template XX to make cutting the strip sets easier. Kaffe has included a photograph of his original quilt to show his inspiration.

CUTTING OUT
Template XX: Cut 1½in (3.75cm) strips across the width of the fabric. Piece the strips into strip sets, with the 'X' fabric in the centre. Use the photograph opposite as a guide to fabric combinations, but don't be tied to

Kaffe's version, enjoy making your own combinations! From each strip set cut 4 squares using Template XX as shown in the cutting diagram. Keep these 4 squares together as they will form a block. Don't worry about lining up the template exactly, a little variation adds charm to the finished blocks. Use the leftovers from the cutting to make extra strip sets, with the addition of an extra strip as shown in the cutting diagram. You will need a total of 195 Template XX squares to complete the quilt centre including the side and bottom inner borders.
Borders: With leftover fabrics (don't use Shot Cotton Coal, SC63) cut strips 4½in (11.5cm) by varying widths, mostly 1½in and 2½in (3.75cm and 6.5cm), and piece 2 side border strips 4½in x 91in (11.5cm x 231.25cm) and 2 top and bottom border strips 4½in x 72in (11.5cm x 183cm).

Binding: Cut 9 strips 2½in (6.5cm) wide across the width of the fabric in WMSFU.

Kaffe's Antique Quilt.

Cutting Diagram

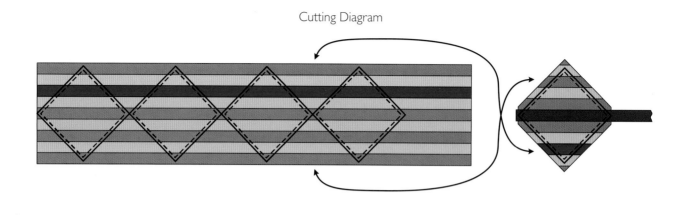

Block Assembly Diagrams

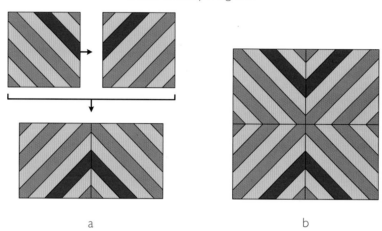

a

b

Backing: Cut 2 pieces 40in × 98in (101.5cm × 249cm) 2 pieces 40in × 8in (101.5cm × 20.5cm) and 1 piece 19in × 8in (48.5cm × 20.5cm) in backing fabric.

MAKING THE BLOCKS AND INNER BORDERS

Use a ¼in (6mm) seam allowance throughout. Using the sets of 4 Template XX squares make up blocks as shown in block assembly diagram a, the 'X' block can be seen in diagram b, make 42. Also piece a right side

inner border strip of 14 Template XX squares and a bottom inner border strip of 13 Template XX squares.

MAKING THE QUILT

Refer to the quilt assembly diagram for fabric placement. Lay out the blocks into 7 rows of 6 blocks. Join the rows, then add the side inner border and the bottom inner border as shown in the quilt assembly diagram. Add the top and bottom pieced borders, then the side pieced borders to complete the quilt.

FINISHING THE QUILT

Press the quilt top. Seam the backing pieces using a ¼in (6mm) seam allowance to form a piece approx. 87in × 98in (221cm × 249cm). Layer the quilt top, batting and backing and baste together (see page 139). Using toning hand quilting thread quilt lines in the 'X' shapes to form a crosshatch pattern across the quilt. Also pick out squares where the blocks intersect and quilt in the centres of the strips. Trim the quilt edges and attach the binding (see page 140).

Quilt Assembly Diagram

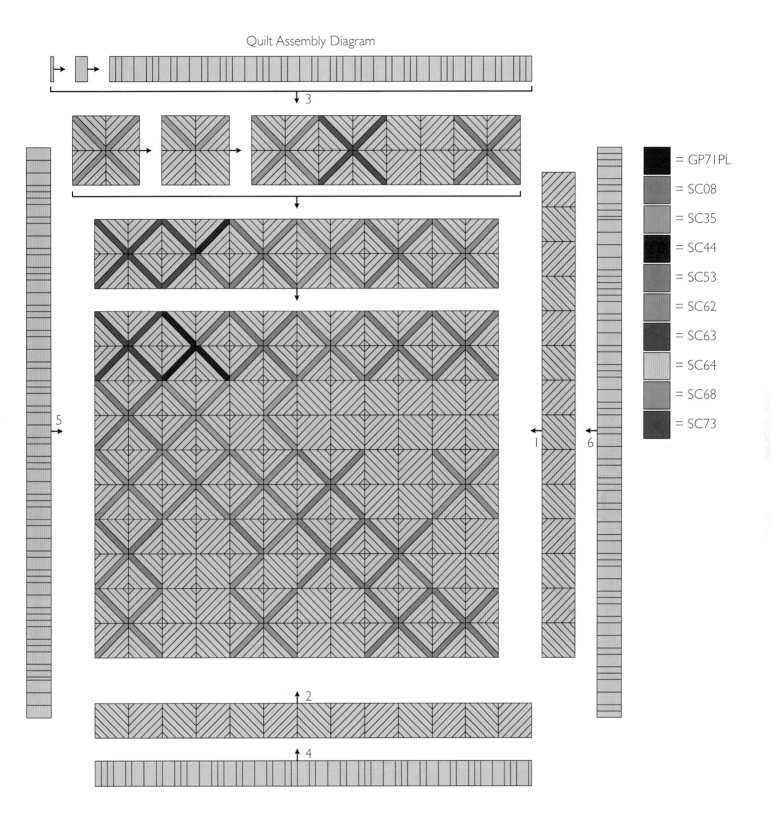

= GP71PL
= SC08
= SC35
= SC44
= SC53
= SC62
= SC63
= SC64
= SC68
= SC73

Fused Flowers on Target Quilt ★★

JUDY BALDWIN

Judy has used Kaffe's Targets fabric as a bold background for her delightful quilt. She has cleverly selected her favourite large blooms in purples and lavenders from the floral fabrics in the collection and appliquéd them liberally over the quilt top. She hopes you have fun making your version.

SIZE OF QUILT

The finished quilt will measure approx. 52½in x 64½in (133.5cm x 164cm).

MATERIALS

Centre Panel:
TARGETS
Pastel   GP67PT: 1¾yds (1.6m)

Borders:
SPOT
Lavender   GP70LV: ⅜yd (35cm)
POMPOM DAHLIAS
Gold   PJ38GD: 1¾yds (1.6m)
           (leftover used in appliqué)

Appliqué Fabrics:
Any large scale floral prints work well in this easy design, buy ½ – ¾yd (45cm – 70cm) of at least 6 fabrics. In this version the following fabrics were used,
BIG BLOOMS Rust, GP91RU
RUSSIAN ROSE Pastel, GP95PT
EMBROIDERED SHAWL Purple, GP106PU
FLORAL BURST Blue, PJ29BL
RAMBLING ROSE Brown, PJ34BR
POMPOM DAHLIAS Gold, PJ38GD (use leftover from borders)

Backing Fabric: 3⅝yds (3.3m)
We suggest these fabrics for backing:
ASIAN CIRCLES Yellow, GP89YE
SPOT Lavender, GP70LV
RUSSIAN ROSE Pastel, GP95PT

Binding:
ABORIGINAL DOTS
Purple   GP71PU: ⅝yd (60cm)

Batting:
60in x 72in (152.5cm x 183cm).

Quilting Thread:
Toning machine quilting thread.

Adhesive Web:
Approx. 3⅜yds (3m) of 17in (44cm) wide lightweight fusible web or equivalent.

PATCH SHAPES

A simple centre panel of fabric is surrounded with an inner and outer border to provide a background for sumptuous floral fused web appliqué.

CUTTING OUT

Centre Panel: Cut a panel 40in x 52in (101.5cm x 132cm) in GP67PT
Inner Border: Cut 5 strips 1½in (3.75cm) wide across the width of the fabric in GP70LV. Join as necessary and cut 2 strips 1½in x 52in (3.75cm x 132cm) for the quilt sides and 2 strips 1½in x 42in (3.75cm x 106.75cm) for the quilt top and bottom.
Outer Border: Cut 4 strips 6in (15.25cm) wide down the length of the fabric (2 from each side along the selvedge, leaving the centre of the fabric for appliqué) in PJ38GD. From these cut 2 strips 6in x 54in (15.25cm x 137.25cm) for the quilt sides and 2 strips 6in x 53in (15.25cm x 134.5cm) for the quilt top and bottom. Reserve the remaining fabric for appliqué.

Binding: Cut 7 strips 2½in (6.5cm) wide across the width of the fabric in GP71PU.

Backing: Cut 1 piece 40in x 60in (101.5cm x 152.5cm) and 1 piece 33in x 60in (84cm x

152.5cm) in backing fabric.

MAKING THE QUILT

Use a ¼in (6mm) seam allowance throughout. Add the inner, then outer borders to the centre panel as shown in the quilt assembly diagram.

ADDING THE APPLIQUÉ

Choose the flowers that you wish to use in each fabric, refer to the photograph for help with this. Apply fusible web to the reverse of each flower, following the manufacturer's instructions and making sure the web is bigger than each flower. Cut out the flowers. Press the quilt well and before removing the paper backing arrange the flowers on the background allowing them to spill over the borders. You may wish to layer some of the flowers, if so cut away the areas which sit behind, leaving a very scant ¼in (6mm) to reduce bulk. Remove the backing papers and fuse the flowers in place. Using matching threads machine stitch the appliqué flowers in place using a fine satin stitch on the very edge of the flowers so that no raw edges are showing.

FINISHING THE QUILT

Press the quilt top. Seam the backing pieces using a ¼in (6mm) seam allowance to form a piece approx. 60in x 72in (152.5cm x 183cm). Layer the quilt top, batting and backing and baste together (see page 139). Using toning thread free motion quilt following the contours of the petals and leaves of the appliqué shapes and in the borders. Also free motion quilt the Targets fabric to create an embossed look. Trim the quilt edges and attach the binding (see page 140).

Quilt Assembly Diagram

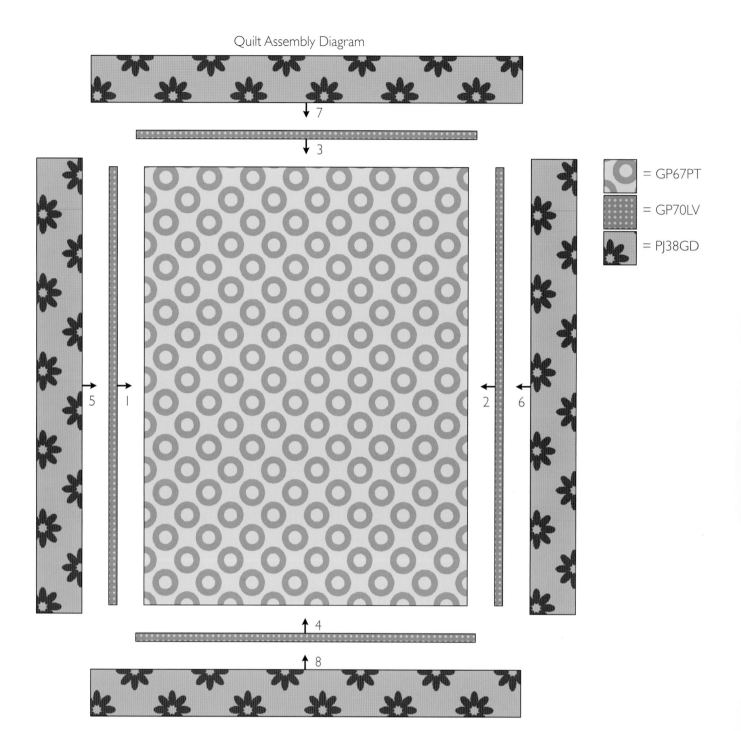

= GP67PT

= GP70LV

= PJ38GD

Templates

Please refer to the individual quilt instructions for the templates required for each quilt as some templates are used in several quilts. The arrows on the templates should be lined up with the straight grain of the fabric, which runs either along the selvedge or at 90 degrees to the selvedge. Following the marked grain lines is important to prevent patches having bias edges along block and quilt edges which can cause distortion. In some quilts the arrows also denote stripe direction.

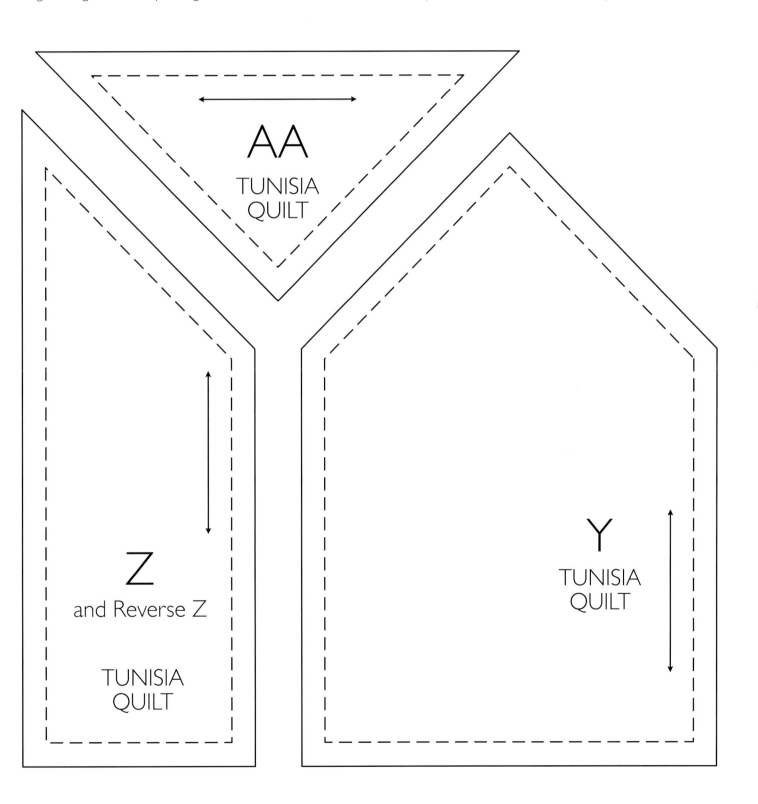

AA
TUNISIA
QUILT

Z
and Reverse Z

TUNISIA
QUILT

Y
TUNISIA
QUILT

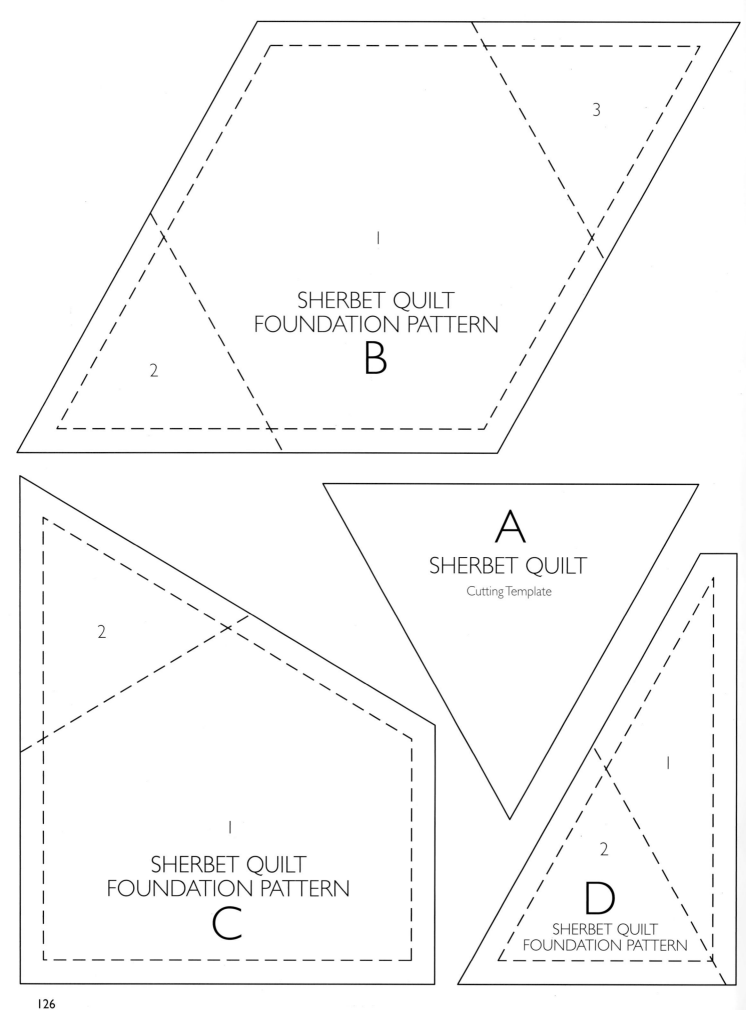

SHERBET QUILT
FOUNDATION PATTERN
B

A
SHERBET QUILT
Cutting Template

SHERBET QUILT
FOUNDATION PATTERN
C

D
SHERBET QUILT
FOUNDATION PATTERN

G
ENCLOSED
4 PATCH
QUILT

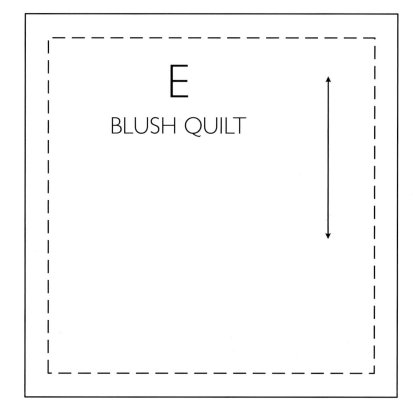

E
BLUSH QUILT

F
ENCLOSED 4 PATCH
QUILT

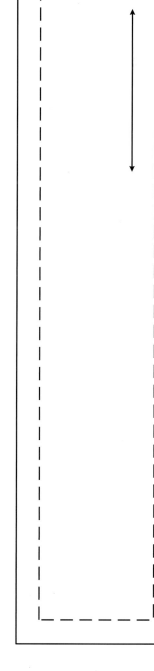

H
ENCLOSED
4 PATCH
QUILT

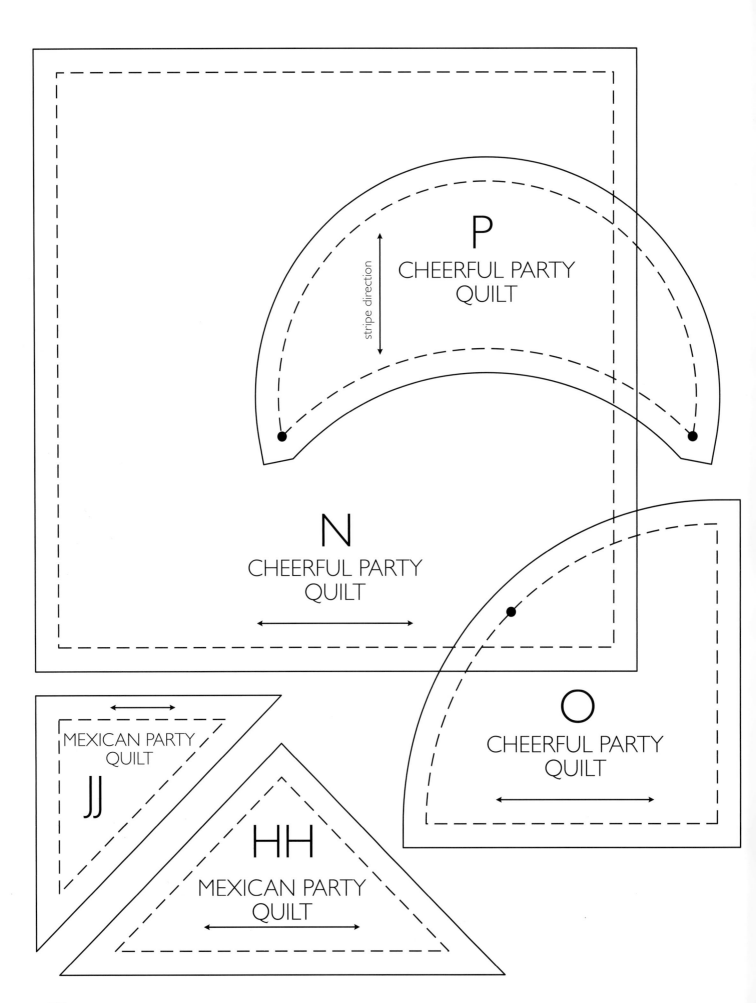

P
CHEERFUL PARTY
QUILT

stripe direction

N
CHEERFUL PARTY
QUILT

O
CHEERFUL PARTY
QUILT

JJ
MEXICAN PARTY
QUILT

HH
MEXICAN PARTY
QUILT

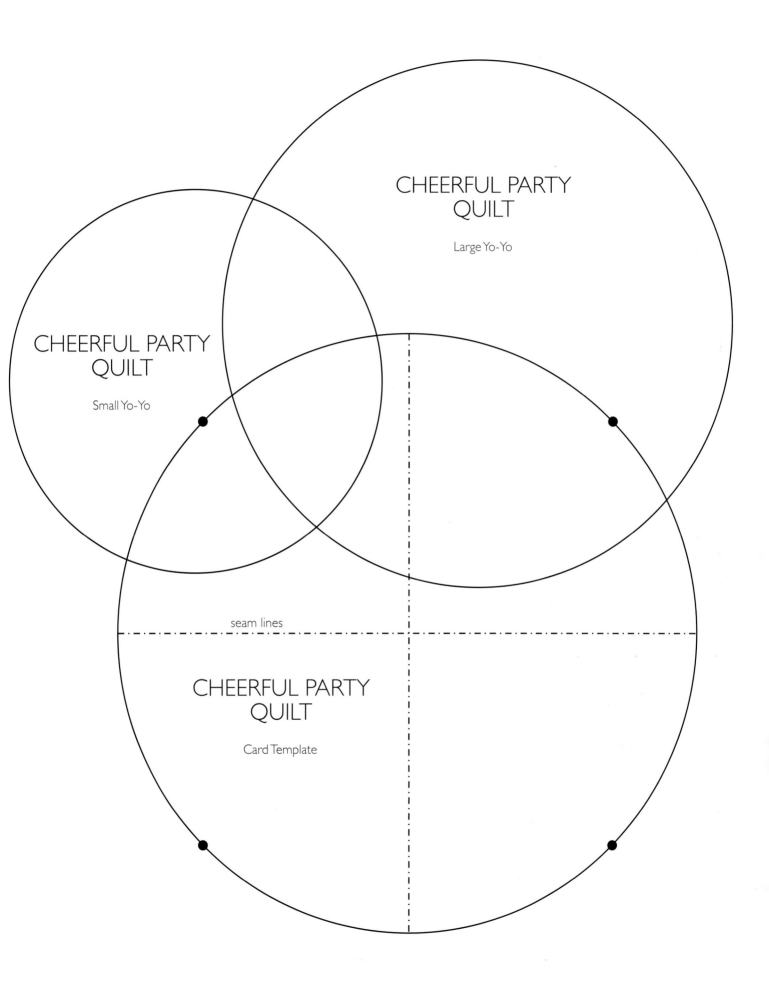

CHEERFUL PARTY
QUILT

Large Yo-Yo

CHEERFUL PARTY
QUILT

Small Yo-Yo

seam lines

CHEERFUL PARTY
QUILT

Card Template

R

GAMEBOARD
QUILT

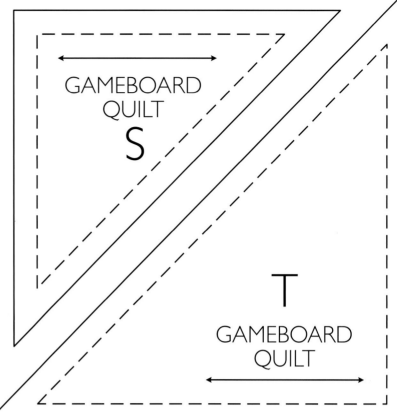

GAMEBOARD
QUILT

S

T

GAMEBOARD
QUILT

SUGAR AND SPICE
SNIPS AND SNAILS
QUILTS

J

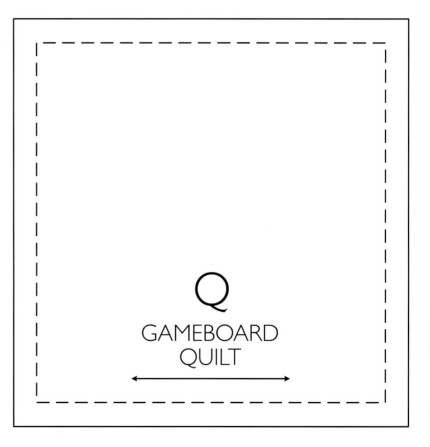

Q

GAMEBOARD
QUILT

GG

MEXICAN PARTY
QUILT

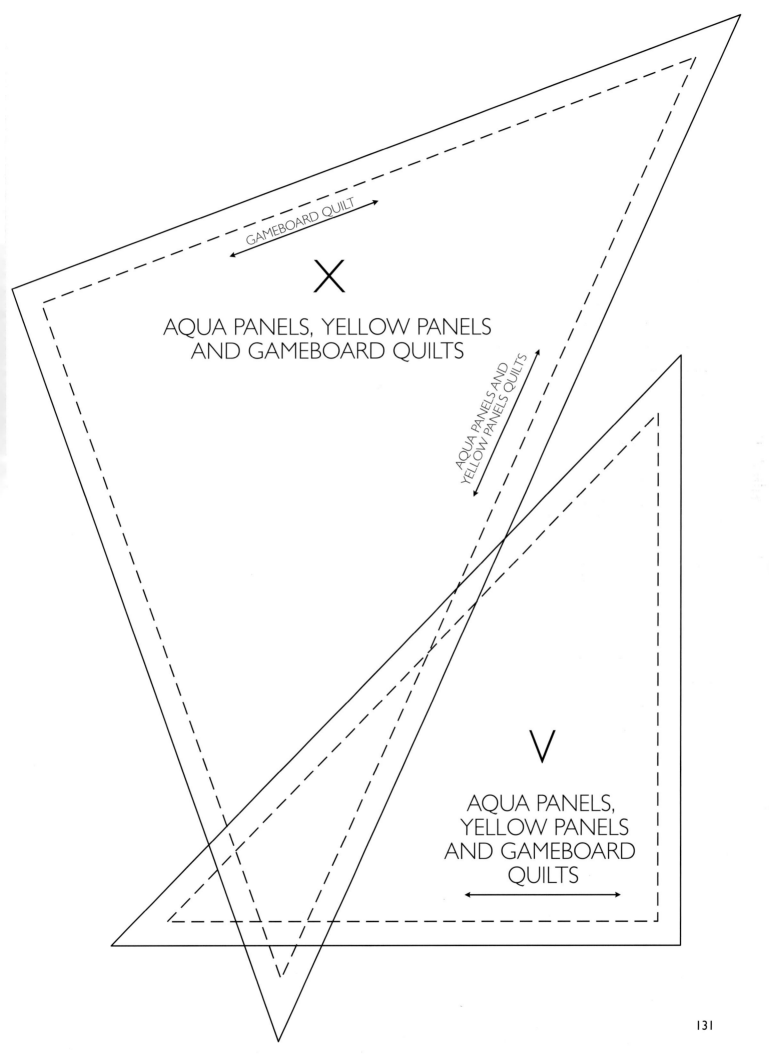

GAMEBOARD QUILT

X

AQUA PANELS, YELLOW PANELS
AND GAMEBOARD QUILTS

AQUA PANELS AND
YELLOW PANELS QUILTS

V

AQUA PANELS,
YELLOW PANELS
AND GAMEBOARD
QUILTS

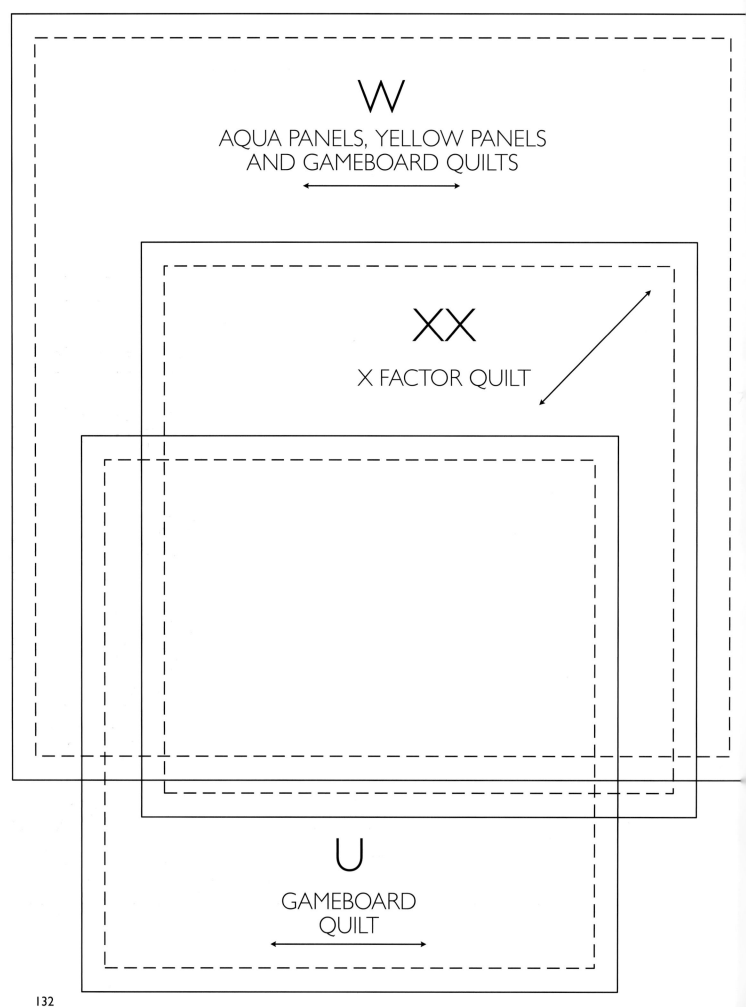

W

AQUA PANELS, YELLOW PANELS
AND GAMEBOARD QUILTS

⟵⟶

XX

X FACTOR QUILT

U

GAMEBOARD
QUILT

⟵⟶

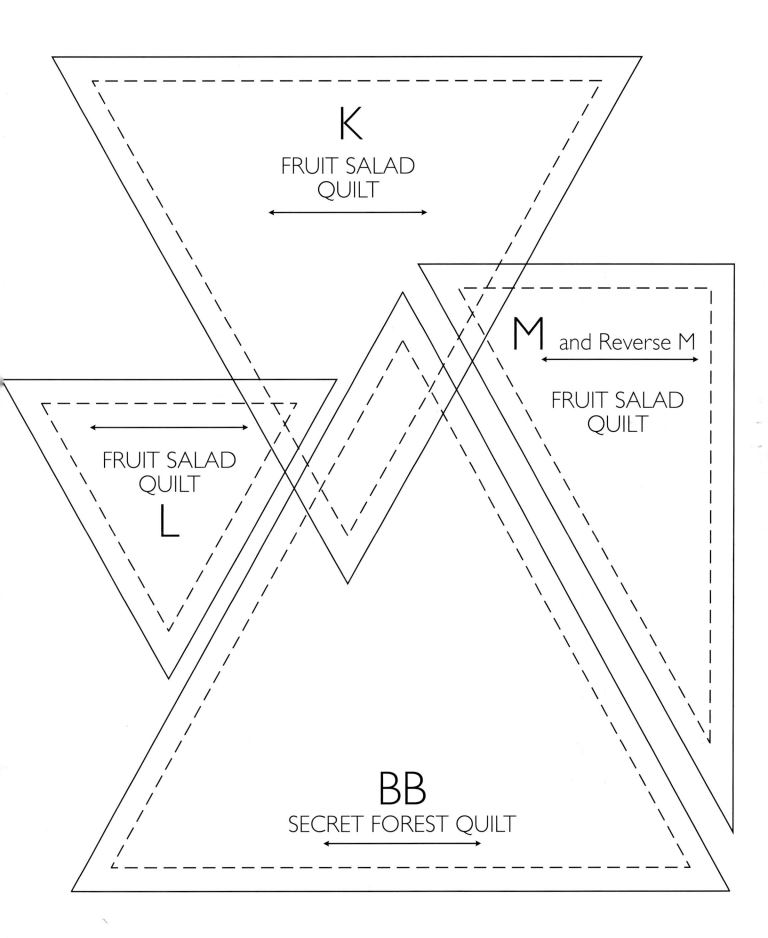

K
FRUIT SALAD
QUILT

M and Reverse M
FRUIT SALAD
QUILT

FRUIT SALAD
QUILT
L

BB
SECRET FOREST QUILT

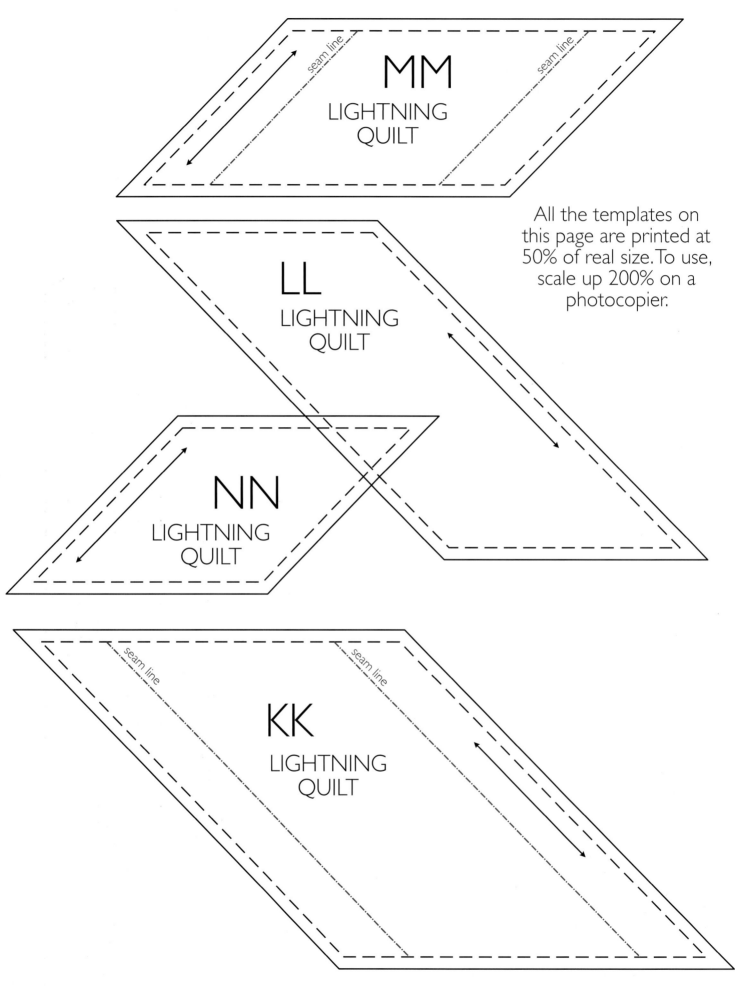

MM
LIGHTNING
QUILT

seam line   *seam line*

All the templates on
this page are printed at
50% of real size. To use,
scale up 200% on a
photocopier.

LL
LIGHTNING
QUILT

NN
LIGHTNING
QUILT

KK
LIGHTNING
QUILT

seam line   *seam line*

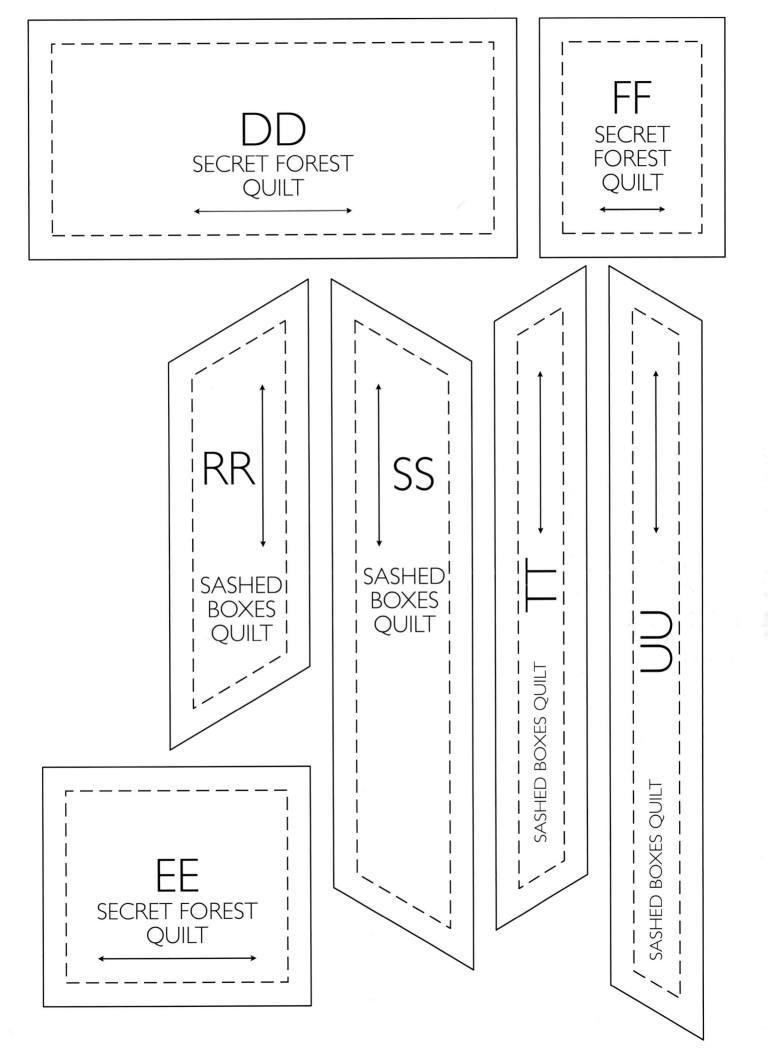

DD
SECRET FOREST
QUILT

FF
SECRET
FOREST
QUILT

RR
SASHED
BOXES
QUILT

SS
SASHED
BOXES
QUILT

TT
SASHED BOXES QUILT

UU
SASHED BOXES QUILT

EE
SECRET FOREST
QUILT

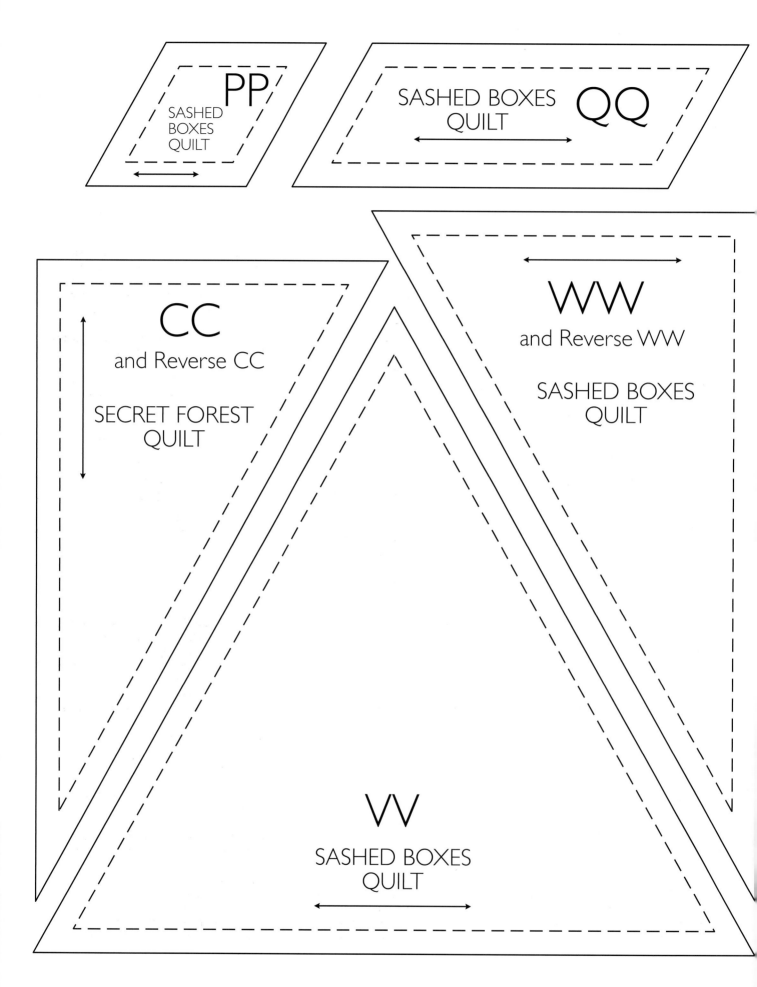

PP
SASHED
BOXES
QUILT

SASHED BOXES
QUILT

QQ

CC
and Reverse CC

SECRET FOREST
QUILT

WW
and Reverse WW

SASHED BOXES
QUILT

VV
SASHED BOXES
QUILT

Patchwork Know How

These instructions are intended for the novice quilt maker, providing the basic information needed to make the projects in this book, along with some useful tips.

Preparing the fabric

Prewash all new fabrics before you begin, to ensure that there will be no uneven shrinkage and no bleeding of colours when the finished quilt is laundered. Press the fabric whilst it is still damp to return crispness to it. All fabric requirements in this book are calculated on a 40in (101.5cm) usable fabric width to allow for shrinkage and selvedge removal.

Making templates

Transparent template plastic is the best material, it is durable and allows you to see the fabric and select certain motifs. You can also use thin stiff cardboard.

Templates for machine piecing

1 Trace off the actual–sized template provided either directly on to template plastic, or tracing paper, and then on to thin cardboard. Use a ruler to help you trace off the straight cutting line, dotted seam line and grain lines. Some of the templates in this book were too large to print at full size, they have therefore been printed at half real size. Photocopy them at 200% before using.

2 Cut out the traced off template using a craft knife, ruler and a self–healing cutting mat.

3 Punch holes in the corners of the template, at each point on the seam line, using a hole punch.

Templates for hand piecing

• Make a template as for machine piecing, but do not trace off the cutting line. Use the dotted seam line as the outer edge of the template.

• This template allows you to draw the seam lines directly on to the fabric. The seam allowances can then be cut by eye around the patch.

Cutting the fabric

On the individual instructions for each patchwork, you will find a summary of all the patch shapes used.
Always mark and cut out any border and binding strips first, followed by the largest patch shapes and finally the smallest ones, to make the most efficient use of your fabric. The border and binding strips are best cut using a rotary cutter.

Rotary cutting

Rotary cut strips are usually cut across the fabric from selvedge to selvedge, but some projects may vary, so please read through all the instructions before you start cutting the fabrics.

1 Before beginning to cut, press out any folds or creases in the fabric. If you are cutting a large piece of fabric, you will need to fold it several times to fit the cutting mat. When there is only a single fold, place the fold facing you. If the fabric is too wide to be folded only once, fold it concertina–style until it fits your mat. A small rotary cutter with a sharp blade will cut up to 6 layers of fabric; a large cutter up to 8 layers.

2 To ensure that your cut strips are straight and even, the folds must be placed exactly parallel to the straight edges of the fabric and along a line on the cutting mat.

3 Place a plastic ruler over the raw edge of the fabric, overlapping it about ½in (1.25cm). Make sure that the ruler is at right angles to both the straight edges and the fold to ensure that you cut along the straight grain. Press down on the ruler and wheel the cutter away from yourself along the edge of the ruler.

4 Open out the fabric to check the edge. Don't worry if it's not perfectly straight, a little wiggle will not show when the quilt is stitched together. Re–fold fabric, then place the ruler over the trimmed edge, aligning edge with the markings on the ruler that match the correct strip width. Cut strip along the edge of the ruler.

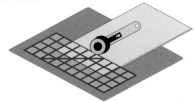

Using templates

The most efficient way to cut out templates is by first rotary cutting a strip of fabric the width stated for your template, and then marking off your templates along the strip, edge to edge at the required angle. This method leaves hardly any waste and gives a random effect to your patches.
A less efficient method is to fussy cut, where the templates are cut individually by placing them on particular motifs or stripes, to create special effects. Although this method is more wasteful it yields very interesting results.

1 Place the template face down, on the wrong side of the fabric, with the grain line arrow following the straight grain of the fabric, if indicated. Be careful though – check with your individual instructions, as some instructions may ask you to cut patches on varying grains.

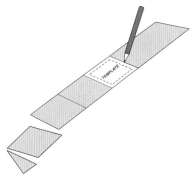

2 Hold the template firmly in place and draw around it with a sharp pencil or crayon, marking in the corner dots or seam lines. To save fabric, position patches close together or even touching. Don't worry if outlines positioned on the straight grain when drawn on striped fabrics do not always match the stripes when cut – this will add a degree of visual excitement to the patchwork!

3 Once you've drawn all the pieces needed, you are ready to cut the fabric, with either a rotary cutter and ruler, or a pair of sharp sewing scissors.

Basic hand and machine piecing

Patches can be joined together by hand or machine. Machine stitching is quicker, but hand assembly allows you to carry your patches around with you and work on them in every spare moment. The choice is yours. For techniques that are new to you, practise on scrap pieces of fabric until you feel confident.

Machine piecing

Follow the quilt instructions for the order in which to piece the individual patchwork blocks and then assemble the blocks together in rows.

1 Seam lines are not marked on the fabric, so stitch ¼in (6mm) seams using the machine needle plate, a ¼in (6mm) wide machine foot, or tape stuck to the machine as a guide. Pin two patches with right sides together, matching edges.

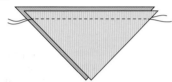

Set your machine at 10–12 stitches per inch (2.5cm) and stitch seams from edge to edge, removing pins as you feed the fabric through the machine.

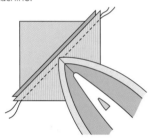

2 Press the seams of each patchwork block to one side before attempting to join it to another block.

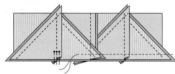

3 When joining rows of blocks, make sure that adjacent seam allowances are pressed in opposite directions to reduce bulk and make matching easier. Pin pieces together directly through the stitch line and to the right and left of the seam. Remove pins as you sew. Continue pressing seams to one side as you work.

Hand piecing

1 Pin two patches with right sides together, so that the marked seam lines are facing outwards.

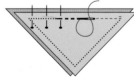

2 Using a single strand of strong thread, secure the corner of a seam line with a couple of back stitches.

3 Sew running stitches along the marked line, working 8–10 stitches per inch (2.5cm) and

ending at the opposite seam line corner with a few back stitches. When hand piecing never stitch over the seam allowances.

4 Press the seams to one side, as shown in machine piecing (Step 2).

Inset seams.

In some patchwork layouts a patch will have to be sewn into an angled corner formed by the joining of two other patches. Use the following method whether you are machine or hand piecing. Don't be intimidated – this is not hard to do once you have learned a couple of techniques. The seam is sewn from the centre outwards in two halves to ensure that no tucks appear at the centre.

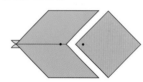

1 Mark with dots exactly where the inset will be joined and mark the seam lines on the wrong side of the fabric on the inset patch.

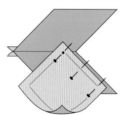

2 With right sides together and inset piece on top, pin through the dots to match the inset points. Pin the rest of the seam at right angles to the stitching line, along one edge of an adjoining patch.

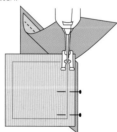

3 Stitch the patch in place along the seam line starting with the needle down through the inset point dots. Secure thread with a backstitch if hand piecing, or stitch forward for a few stitches before backstitching, when machine piecing.

4 Pivot the patch, to enable it to align with the adjacent side of the angled corner, allowing you work on the second half of the seam. Starting with a pin at the inset point once again. Pin and stitch the second side in place, as before. Check seams and press carefully.

Machine appliqué
Using adhesive web:

To make appliqué very easy you can use adhesive web, which comes attached to a paper backing sheet, to bond the motifs to the background fabric. There are 2 types of web available, the first keeps the pieces in place whilst they are stitched, the second permanently attaches the pieces so that no sewing is required. Follow steps 1 and 2 for the non–sew type and steps 1–3 for the type that requires sewing.

1 Trace the reversed appliqué design onto the paper side of the adhesive web leaving a ¼in (6mm) gap between all the shapes. Roughly cut out the motifs ⅛in (3mm) outside your drawn line.

2 Bond the motifs to the reverse of your chosen fabrics. Cut out on the drawn line with very sharp scissors. Remove the backing paper by scoring in the centre of the motif carefully with a scissor point and peeling the paper away from the centre out, this prevents damage to the edges. Place the motifs onto the background noting any which may be layered. Cover with a clean cloth and bond with a hot iron (check instructions for temperature setting as adhesive web can vary depending on the manufacturer).

3 Using a contrasting or complimenting coloured thread in your machine, work small close zigzag stitches or a blanket stitch if your machine has one, around the edge of the motifs, the majority of the stitching should sit on the appliqué shape. When stitching up to points stop with the machine needle in the down position, lift the foot of your machine, pivot the work, lower the foot and continue to stitch. Make sure all the raw edges are stitched.

Hand appliqué

Good preparation is essential for speedy and accurate hand appliqué. The finger–pressing method is suitable for needle–turning application, used for simple shapes like leaves and flowers. Using a card template is the best method for bold simple motifs such as circles.

Finger–pressing:

1 To make your template, transfer the appliqué design on to stiff card using carbon paper, and cut out template. Trace around the outline of your appliquéd shape on to the right

side of your fabric using a well sharpened pencil. Cut out shapes, adding a ¼in (6mm) seam allowance all around by eye.

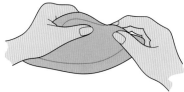

2 Hold shape right side up and fold under the seam, turning along your drawn line, pinch to form a crease. Dampening the fabric makes this very easy. When using shapes with 'points' such as leaves turn the seam allowance at the 'point' in first as shown in the diagram, then continue all round the shape. If your shapes have sharp curves you can snip the seam allowance to ease the curve. Take care not to stretch the appliqué shapes as you work.

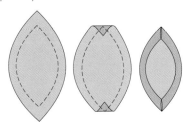

Card templates:

1 Cut out appliqué shapes as shown in step 1 of finger–pressing. Make a circular template from thin cardboard, without seam allowances.

2 Using a matching thread, work a row of running stitches close to the edge of the fabric circle. Place thin cardboard template in the centre of the fabric circle on the wrong side of the fabric.

3 Carefully pull up the running stitches to gather up the edge of the fabric circle around the cardboard template. Press, so that no puckers or tucks appear on the right side. Then, carefully pop out the cardboard template without distorting the fabric shape.

Needle–turning application

1 Take the appliqué shape and pin in position. Stroke the seam allowance under with the tip of the needle as far as the creased pencil line, and hold securely in place with your thumb. Using a matching thread, bring the needle up from the back of the block into the edge of the shape and proceed to blind–hem in place. This is a stitch where the motifs appear to be held on invisibly. Bring the thread out from below through the folded edge of the motif, never on the top. The stitches must be worked small, even and close together to prevent the seam allowance from unfolding and frayed edges appearing. Try to avoid pulling the stitches too tight, as this will cause the motifs to pucker up. Work around the whole shape, stroking under each small section before sewing.

Quilting and finishing

When you have finished piecing your patchwork and added any borders, press it carefully. It is now ready for quilting.

Marking quilting designs and motifs

Many tools are available for marking quilting patterns, check the manufacturer's instructions for use and test on scraps of fabric from your project. Use an acrylic ruler for marking straight lines.

Stencils: Some designs require stencils, these can be made at home, by transferring the designs on to template plastic, or stiff cardboard. The design is then cut away in the form of long dashes, to act as guides for both internal and external lines. These stencils are a quick method for producing an identical set of repeated designs.

Preparing the backing and batting

• Remove the selvedges and piece together the backing fabric to form a backing at least 4in (10cm) larger all round than the patchwork top.

• For quilting choose a fairly thin batting, preferably pure cotton, to give your quilt a flat appearance. If your batting has been rolled up, unroll it and let it rest before cutting it to the same size as the backing.

• For a large quilt it may be necessary to join 2 pieces of batting to fit. Lay the pieces of batting on

a flat surface so that they overlap by approx. 8in (20cm). Cut a curved line through both layers.

overlap wadding

• Carefully peel away the two narrow pieces and discard. Butt the curved cut edges back together. Stitch the two pieces together using a large herringbone stitch.

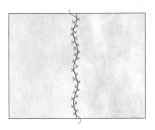

Basting the layers together

1 On a bare floor or large work surface, lay out the backing with wrong side uppermost. Use weights along the edges to keep it taut.

2 Lay the batting on the backing and smooth it out gently. Next lay the patchwork top, right side up, on top of the batting and smooth gently until there are no wrinkles. Pin at the corners and at the midpoints of each side, close to the edges.

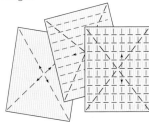

3 Beginning at the centre, baste diagonal lines outwards to the corners, making your stitches about 3in (7.5cm) long. Then, again starting at the centre, baste horizontal and vertical lines out to the edges. Continue basting until you have basted a grid of lines about 4in (10cm) apart over the entire quilt.

4 For speed, when machine quilting, some quilters prefer to baste their quilt sandwich layers together using rust–proof safety pins, spaced at 4in (10cm) intervals over the entire quilt.

Hand quilting

This is best done with the quilt mounted on a quilting frame or hoop, but as long as you have basted the quilt well, a frame is not essential. With the quilt top facing upwards, begin at the centre of the quilt and make even running stitches following the design. It is more important to make even stitches on both sides of the quilt than to make small ones. Start and finish your stitching with back stitches and bury the ends of your threads in the batting.

Machine quilting

• For a flat looking quilt, always use a walking foot on your machine for straight lines, and a darning foot for free–motion quilting.

• It's best to start your quilting at the centre of the quilt and work out towards the borders, doing the straight quilting lines first (stitch–in–the–ditch) followed by the free–motion quilting.

• When free motion quilting stitch in a loose meandering style as shown in the diagrams. Do not stitch too closely as this will make the quilt feel stiff when finished. If you wish you can include floral themes or follow shapes on the printed fabrics for added interest.

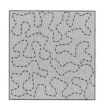

• Make it easier for yourself by handling the quilt properly. Roll up the excess quilt neatly to fit under your sewing machine arm, and use a table, or chair to help support the weight of the quilt that hangs down the other side.

Preparing to bind the edges

Once you have quilted or tied your quilt sandwich together, remove all the basting stitches. Then, baste around the outer edge of the quilt ¼in (6mm) from the edge of the top patchwork layer. Trim the back and batting to the edge of the patchwork and straighten the edge of the patchwork if necessary.

Making the binding

1 Cut bias or straight grain strips the width required for your binding, making sure the grainline is running the correct way on your straight grain strips. Cut enough strips until you have the required length to go around the edge of your quilt.

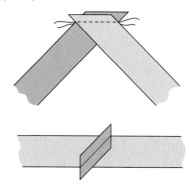

2 To join strips together, the two ends that are to be joined must be cut at a 45 degree angle, as above. Stitch right sides together, trim turnings and press seam open.

Binding the edges

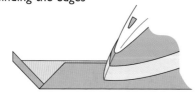

1 Cut the starting end of binding strip at a 45 degree angle, fold a ¼in (6mm) turning to wrong side along cut edge and press in place. With wrong sides together, fold strip in half lengthways, keeping raw edges level, and press.

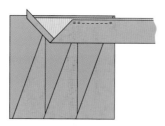

2 Starting at the centre of one of the long edges, place the doubled binding on to the right side of the quilt keeping raw edges level. Stitch the binding in place starting ¼in (6mm) in from the diagonal folded edge (see above). Reverse stitch to secure, and working ¼in (6mm) in from edge of the quilt towards first corner of quilt. Stop ¼in (6mm) in from corner and work a few reverse stitches.

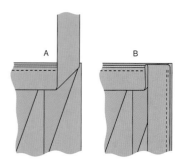

3 Fold the loose end of the binding up, making a 45 degree angle (see A). Keeping the diagonal fold in place, fold the binding back down, aligning the raw edges with the next side of the quilt. Starting at the point where the last stitch ended, stitch down the next side (see B).

4 Continue to stitch the binding in place around all the quilt edges in this way, tucking the finishing end of the binding inside the diagonal starting section (see above).

5 Turn the folded edge of the binding on to the back of the quilt. Hand stitch the folded edge in place just covering binding machine stitches, and folding a mitre at each corner.

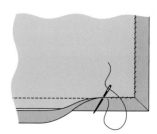

Glossary of Terms

Adhesive web see fusible web

Appliqué The technique of stitching fabric shapes on to a background to create a design. It can be applied either by hand or machine with a decorative embroidery stitch, such as buttonhole, or satin stitch.

Backing The bottom layer of a quilt sandwich. It is made of fabric pieced to the size of the quilt top with the addition of about 3in (7.5cm) all around to allow for quilting take–up.

Basting or Tacking This is a means of holding two fabric layers or the layers of a quilt sandwich together temporarily with large hand stitches, or pins.

Batting or Wadding This is the middle layer, or padding in a quilt. It can be made of cotton, wool, silk or synthetic fibres.

Bias The diagonal grain of a fabric. This is the direction which has the most give or stretch, making it ideal for bindings, especially on curved edges.

Binding A narrow strip of fabric used to finish off the edges of quilts or projects; it can be cut on the straight grain of a fabric or on the bias.

Block A single design unit that when stitched together with other blocks create the quilt top. It is most often a square, hexagon, or rectangle, but it can be any shape. It can be pieced or plain.

Border A frame of fabric stitched to the outer edges of the quilt top. Borders can be narrow or wide, pieced or plain. As well as making the quilt larger, they unify the overall design and draw attention to the central area.

Chalk pencils Available in various colours, they are used for marking lines, or spots on fabric.

Cutting mat Designed for use with a rotary cutter, it is made from a special 'self–healing' material that keeps your cutting blade sharp. Cutting mats come in various sizes and are usually marked with a grid to help you line up the edges of fabric and cut out larger pieces.

Design Wall Used for laying out fabric patches before sewing. A large wall or folding board covered with flannel fabric or cotton batting in a neutral shade (dull beige or grey work well) will hold fabric in place so that an overall view can be taken of the placement.

Free–motion quilting Curved wavy quilting lines stitched in a random manner. Stitching diagrams are often given for you to follow as a loose guide.

Freezer Paper Paper which is plasticized on one side, usually sold on a roll. Originally used for wrapping meat for freezing it was found to adhere to fabric when pressed. It is useful for appliqué as it stays in place until peeled away without leaving any residue.

Fusible web Adhesive web, which comes attached to a paper backing sheet, used to bond appliqué motifs to a background fabric. There are 2 types of web available, the first keeps the pieces in place whilst they are stitched, the second permanently attaches the pieces so that no sewing is required.

Fussy cutting This is when a template is placed on a particular motif, or stripe, to obtain interesting effects. This method is not as efficient as strip cutting, but yields very interesting results.

Grain The direction in which the threads run in a woven fabric. In a vertical direction it is called the lengthwise grain, which has very little stretch. The horizontal direction, or crosswise grain is slightly stretchy, but diagonally the fabric has a lot of stretch. This grain is called the bias. Wherever possible the grain of a fabric should run in the same direction on a quilt block and borders.

Grain Lines These are arrows printed on templates which should be aligned with the fabric grain.

Inset seams or setting–in A patchwork technique whereby one patch (or block) is stitched into a 'V' shape formed by the joining of two other patches (or blocks).

Patch A small shaped piece of fabric used in the making of a patchwork pattern.

Patchwork The technique of stitching small pieces of fabric (patches) together to create a larger piece of fabric, usually forming a design.

Pieced quilt A quilt composed of patches.

Quilting Traditionally done by hand with running stitches, but for speed modern quilts are often stitched by machine. The stitches are sewn through the top, wadding and backing to hold the three layers together. Quilting stitches are usually worked in some form of design, but they can be random.

Quilting hoop Consists of two wooden circular or oval rings with a screw adjuster on the outer ring.

It stabilises the quilt layers, helping to create an even tension.

Rotary cutter A sharp circular blade attached to a handle for quick, accurate cutting. It is a device that can be used to cut up to six layers of fabric at one time. It must be used in conjunction with a 'self–healing' cutting mat and a thick plastic ruler.

Rotary ruler A thick, clear plastic ruler printed with lines that are exactly ¼in (6mm) apart. Sometimes they also have diagonal lines printed on, indicating 45 and 60 degree angles. A rotary ruler is used as a guide when cutting out fabric pieces using a rotary cutter.

Sashing A piece or pieced sections of fabric interspaced between blocks.

Sashing Posts When blocks have sashing between them the corner squares are known as sashing posts.

Selvedges Also known as selvages, these are the firmly woven edges down each side of a fabric length. Selvedges should be trimmed off before cutting out your fabric, as they are more liable to shrink when the fabric is washed.

Stitch–in–the–ditch or Ditch quilting Also known as quilting–in–the–ditch. The quilting stitches are worked along the actual seam lines, to give a pieced quilt texture.

Template A pattern piece used as a guide for marking and cutting out fabric patches, or marking a quilting, or appliqué design. Usually made from plastic or strong card that can be reused many times. Templates for cutting fabric usually have marked grain lines which should be aligned with the fabric grain.

Threads One hundred percent cotton or cotton–covered polyester is best for hand and machine piecing. Choose a colour that matches your fabric. When sewing different colours and patterns together, choose a medium to light neutral colour, such as grey or ecru. Specialist quilting threads are available for hand and machine quilting.

Walking foot or Quilting foot This is a sewing machine foot with dual feed control. It is very helpful when quilting, as the fabric layers are fed evenly from the top and below, reducing the risk of slippage and puckering.

Yo-Yos A circle of fabric double the size of the finished puff is gathered up into a rosette shape.

Biographies

Judy Baldwin

A retired elementary school teacher, Judy began quilting more than 30 years ago. The bicentennial had created new interest in quilting and quilt stores began to appear nearby. When a friend opened a quilt store Judy began working for her and taking classes, with quilting becoming her main interest. Within a few years she became the manager. Occasionally Liza and Kaffe would drop in and they became friends. As Liza's online business began to grow, Judy joined the small crew who helped make "Glorious Color" a thriving business.

Pauline Smith

Pauline Smith has been a quilt maker and designer since a college visit to The American Museum in Bath in 1968. She makes most of Kaffe's quilts for the Rowan Patchwork And Quilting books, and as the Rowan patchwork co-ordinator, she works closely with everyone involved in producing the 'Patchwork and Quilting' series.

Sally Davis

Sally began quiltmaking in 1980 after experimenting with every known craft. It quickly became a love affair and passion. Sally owned a quilt shop called Quilt Connection where she met Liza and Kaffe and over 9 years encompassed her love of colour with their style and fabrics. Two of her quilts were featured in Rowan P&Q 4 and a Colourful Journey. After closing the store 2 years ago, Sally has been travelling around the country teaching and lecturing as well as working with Liza.

Roberta Horton

Roberta Horton of Berkeley, California has been a quiltmaker for over 30 years. She has taught and lectured worldwide. Her study and love of quilts has pushed her into developing many workshops and to the authoring of six books. Roberta was the recipient of the 2000 Silver Star Award presented by the International Quilt Association. This was in recognition of her lifetime body of work and the long-term effect it has had on quilting.

Brandon Mably

A regular contributor to the Rowan Patchwork books Brandon Mably has built a reputation as a quilt designer of simple, elegant quilts in restful colours. Brandon trained at The Kaffe Fassett Studio. He designs for the Rowan and Vogue Knitting magazine knitwear collections, and is the author of *Brilliant Knits* and *Knitting Color*. Brandon launched his first fabric designs for Rowan in 2008.

Mary Mashuta

California quiltmaker Mary Mashuta has been making quilts and wearables for over thirty years. She is a professionally trained teacher who has been teaching internationally since 1985. Her classes always stress easily understood colour and design. She knows that no quilter can own too much fabric, and she enjoys discovering new blocks to showcase personal collections. Mary has authored six books, the latest is *Foolproof Machine Quilting* and numerous magazine articles.

Ruth Eglinton

Ruth's first job was in banking and her ability with numbers, computers and organisation was born there. After getting married, she took up dressmaking for her little girls and it was during a shopping trip for fabric that she met her great friend Maggie Wise. Maggie was the catalyst that launched Ruth into the quilting world. After a while Ruth discovered the 'mathematics' of quilt making is her real fair and embarked on a new career in technical editing and illustrating, combining her ability with computers with her love of all things fabric. She first worked with a British quilting magazine, then since 2001 with Rowan.

Liza Prior Lucy

Liza Prior Lucy first began making quilts in 1990. She was so enthralled by the craftspeople she met and by the generously stocked quilt fabric shops in the States that quiltmaking soon became a passion. Liza originally trained as a knitwear designer and produced features for needlework magazines. She also owned and operated her own needlepoint shop in Washington, D.C.

Liza met Kaffe when she was working as a sales representative for Rowan Yarns. They worked closely together to write and produce the quilts for the books Glorious Patchwork, Passionate Patchwork and Kaffe Fassett's V&A Quilts.

Experience Ratings

★ Easy, straightforward, suitable for a beginner.

★ ★ Suitable for the average patchworker and quilter.

★ ★ ★ For the more experienced patchworker and quilter.

Other ROWAN Titles Available

Patchwork And Quilting Book 4
A Colourful Journey
Kaffe Fassett's Quilt Road
Kaffe Fassett's Quilts In The Sun
Kaffe Fassett's Country Garden Quilts
Kaffe Fassett's Quilt Romance

Printed Fabrics

When ordering printed fabrics please note the following codes which
precede the fabric number and two digit colour code.
GP is the code for the Kaffe Fassett collection
PJ is the code for the Philip Jacobs collection
BM is the code for the Brandon Mably collection

The fabric collection can be viewed online at the following
www.westminsterfibers.com

All machine threads, Anchor embroidery threads, and Prym sewing aids, distributed in UK by Coats Crafts UK, P.O. Box 22, Lingfield House, Lingfield
Point, McMullen Road, Darlington, Co. Durham, DL1 1YQ.
Consumer helpline: 01325 394237.

Anchor embroidery thread and Coats sewing threads, distributed in the USA by Coats & Clark,
3430 Toringdon Way, Charlotte, North Carolina 28277.
Tel: 704 329 5800. • Fax: 704 329 5027.

Prym products distributed in the USA by Prym-Dritz Corp,
950 Brisack Road, Spartanburg, SC 29303.
Tel: +1 864 576 5050 • Fax: +1 864 587 3353,
e-mail: pdmar@teleplex.net

Green Lane Mill, Holmfirth, West Yorkshire, England
Tel: +44 (0) 1484 681881 • Fax: +44 (0) 1484 6879201 • Internet: www.knitrowan.com
Email: mail@knitrowan.com

Distributors and Stockists
Overseas Distributors of Rowan Fabrics

AUSTRIA
Rhinetex
Geurdeland 7
6673 DR Andelst
The Netherlands
Tel: 31 488 480030
Email: info@rhinetex.com

AUSTRALIA
XLN Fabrics
2/21 Binney Road,
Kings Park
New South Wales 2148
Tel: 61-2 -9621-3066
Email: info@xln.co.zu

BELGIUM
Rhinetex
Geurdeland 7
6673 DR Andelst
The Netherlands
Tel: 31- 488- 480030
Email: info@rhinetex.com

BRAZIL
Coats Corrente Ltd
Rua Do Manifesto,
705 Ipiranga
Sao Paulo
SP 04209-00
Tel: 5511-3247-8000

BULGARIA, GREECE, CYPRUS
Coats Bulgaria EOOD
7 Magnaurska shkola Str.
1784 Sofia, Bulgaria
Tel: +359 2 976 77 41-45
Fax: +359 2 976 77 20
Email: officebg@coats.com
BG: www.coatsbulgaria.bg
GR: www.coatscrafts.gr
CY: www.coatscrafts.com.cy

CANADA
Telio
625 Rue DesLauriers
Montreal, QC, Canada
Tel: 514- 271- 4607
Email: info@telio.com

CZECH REPUBLIC
Coats Czecho s.r.o.
Staré Mesto 246
56932 Staré Mesto
Czech Republic
Tel: 00420 461 616633
Fax: 00420 461 542544
Email: galanterie@coats.com
www.coatscrafts.cz

DENMARK
Coats Expotex AB
Box 297
SE-401 24 Goteborg
Tel: -+46 31 72145-15
Fax: +46 31 471650

FINLAND
Coats Opti Crafts Oy
Ketjutie 3
04220 Kerava
Finland
Tel: 358-9-274871

FRANCE
Rhinetex
Geurdeland 7
6673 DR Andelst
The Netherlands
Tel: 31 488 480 0 30
Email: info@rhinetex.com

GERMANY
Rhinetex
Geurdeland 7
6673 DR Andelst
The Netherlands
Tel: 31 488 480030
Email: info@rhinetex.com

HUNGARY
Coats Crafts Hungary Kft.
H-7500 Nagyatad
Gyar utca 21.
www.coatscrafts.hu

ITALY
Coats Cucirini Srl
Viale Sarca 223
20126 Milano Mi
MILANO

JAPAN
Kiyohara & Co Ltd
4-5-2 Minamikyuhoji-Machi
Chuo-Ku
OSAKA
541-8506
Tel: 81 6 6251 7179

KOREA
Coats Korea Co Ltd,
5F Kuckdong B/D,
935-40 Bangbae-Dong,
Seocho-Gu, Seoul,
South Korea
Tel: 82- 2 -521- 6262

LATVIA
Coats Latvija SIA
Mükusalas iela 41 b
Rïga LV-1004
Latvia
Tel: +371 7 625173
Fax: +371 7 892758
Email: info@coats.lv
www.coatscrafts.lv

LITHUANIA
Coats Lietuva UAB
A.Juozapaviciaus g. 6/2,
LT-09310 Vilinius
Tel: 3705- 2730972
Fax: 3705 2723057
www.coatscrafts.lt

LUXEMBOURG
Rhinetex
Geurdeland 7
6673 DR Andelst
The Netherlands
Tel: 31 488 480 0 30
Email: info@rhinetex.com

NEW ZEALAND
Fabco Limited
280 School Road
P.O. Box 84-002
Westgate
AUCKLAND 1250
Tel: 64- 9- 411- 9996
Email: info@fabco.co.nz

NETHERLANDS
Rhinetex
Geurdeland 7
6673 DR Andelst
The Netherlands
Tel: 31 488 480 0 30
Email: info@rhinetex.com

NORWAY
Coats Expotex AB
Box 297
SE-401 24 Goteborg
Tel: +46 31 7214515
Fax: +46 31 471650

POLAND
Coats Polska Sp.z.o.o
ul. Kaczencowa 16
91-214 Lodz
Tel: 48 42 254 0400
www.coatscrafts.pl

PORTUGAL
Companhia de Linha Coats & Clark, SA
Quinta de Cravel
4430-968 Vila Nova de Gaia
Tel: 00 351- 223 770 700

SINGAPORE
Quilts and Calicos
163 Tanglin Road
03-13 Tanglin Mall
247933
Tel: 65- 688 74708

SLOVAK REPUBLIC
Coats s.r.o.
Kopcianska 94
85101 Bratislava
Slovak Republic
Te: 00421 2 63532314
Fax: 00421 2 63537714
Email: galanteria@coats.com
www.coatscrafts.sk

SOUTH AFRICA
Arthur Bales PTY Ltd
62 4th Avenue
PO Box 44644
Linden 2104
Tel: 27- 11- 888- 2401

SPAIN
Coats Fabra, S.A.
Sant Adria, 20
E-08030 Barcelona
Tel: 00 +34 93- 290. 84. 00
Fax: +34 93-290.84.39

SWITZERLAND
Rhinetex
Geurdeland 7
6673 DR Andelst
The Netherlands
Tel: 31 488 480030
Email: info@rhinetex.com

SWEDEN
Coats Expotex AB
Box 297
SE-401 24 Goteborg
Tel: +46 31 7214515
Fax: +46 31 471650

TAIWAN
Long Teh Trading Co
3F N0 19-2 Kung Yuan Road
Taichung, Taiwan
Tel: 886-4-225-6698

UK
Rowan
Green Lane Mill
Holmfirth
HD9 2DX
United Kingdom
Tel: +44(0) 1484 681881
Email: mail@knitrowan.com
www.knitrowan.com

U.S.A
Westminster Fibers
3430 Toringdon Way
Suite 301,
Charlotte,
NC 28277
Tel: 704-329-5822
Email: fabric@westminsterfibers.com
www.westminsterfibers.com